# THE FORGOTTEN FIFTH

*The Nathan I. Huggins Lectures*

# THE

# FORGOTTEN FIFTH

*African Americans*
*in the Age of Revolution*

## Gary B. Nash

HARVARD UNIVERSITY PRESS
Cambridge, Massachusetts, and London, England
2006

*Library of Congress Cataloging-in-Publication Data*

Nash, Gary B.

The forgotten fifth : African Americans in the age of revolution /
Gary B. Nash.

p. cm.

Based on the Nathan I. Huggins lectures given at the Du Bois
Institute, Harvard University, on Nov. 8–10, 2004.

Includes bibliographical references (p.   ) and index.

ISBN 0-674-02193-2 (alk. paper)

1. United States—History—Revolution, 1775–1783—African
Americans—Congresses.   2. African Americans—History—To 1863—
Congresses.   3. Slavery—United States—History—18th century—
Congresses.   4. United States—Race relations—History—
18th century—Congresses.   5. United States—Race relations—
History—19th century—Congresses.   I. Title.

E269.N3N36 2006
326.0973′09033—dc22                    2005052692

# CONTENTS

# PREFACE

OVER THE LAST four decades, one of my greatest satisfactions in being an historian is to have figured among those working to construct a more democratically conceived American history—one that strives to portray a richly diverse people in a country that has seen one storm of strangers after another landing on its shores. Years ago, the English historian J. H. Plumb spoke of the need to move away from "confirmatory history"—a "narration of events of *particular* people, nations, or communities in order to justify authority, to create confidence, and to secure stability" among society's power holders. My goal in writing history has not been to destabilize history but rather to bring attention to those forgotten Americans who have inarguably been part of constructing our society and our nation.

Among those people who have returned to the stage of history through the efforts of hundreds of historians are African Americans. All of us who have joyously worked to restore black Americans to our national narrative are indebted to W. E. B. Du Bois, Carter Woodson, Rayford Logan, Herbert Aptheker, Philip Foner, Benjamin Quarles, John Hope Franklin, and others who were the lonely sentinels of African American history in the first two-thirds of the twentieth century. Then came the explosion of scholarly interest in what had surely been the most demeaned and neglected part of American society.

It was a special day in July 2002 when Henry Louis Gates Jr., W. E. B. Du Bois Professor of the Humanities and Director of the Du Bois Institute for African and African American Research at Harvard University, invited me to give the Nathan I. Huggins Lectures in 2004. I had known and greatly admired Nathan Huggins when he taught at the University of California, Berkeley, before accepting one of the first appointments in the Du Bois Institute. He made major contributions to American history and was in the middle of a biography of Ralph Bunche when his untimely death took him from us. I hope he would have liked the chapters that follow, which are extended versions of the lectures I gave at the Du Bois Institute on November 8–10, 2004.

In Professor Gates's absence on that occasion, Professor Evelyn Higginbotham extended warm hospitality, a gracious introduction, and stimulating dinners. The astute comments and probing questions of those who attended the lectures have contributed to and improved this book. I am indebted as well to friends and colleagues who read and offered advice on some or all of the chapters: Joyce Appleby, Bert Nanus, Dick Longaker, and Joel Aberbach. Joyce Seltzer and Camille Smith of Harvard University Press helped me reshape the lectures for publication. Marian Olivas at the National Center for History in the Schools at UCLA provided editorial and technical assistance.

# THE FORGOTTEN FIFTH

# 1

## THE BLACK AMERICANS' REVOLUTION

IN THE CENTURIES-LONG HISTORY of Africans in America, the struggle for freedom and equality has suffused the black experience. Gaining freedom in a land of captivity and wresting equality from a society whose founding documents guarantee it has been the consuming desire and everlasting hope that has kept harrowed bodies and weary souls going. In this struggle to cross the river from bondage to liberty, the American Revolution had enormous importance. It marked the first mass slave rebellion in American history, initiated the first civil rights movement, produced the first reconstruction of black life, brought forth the first written testimonies from African Americans who wanted the world to hear of their strivings and their claims to freedom, and involved the first budding of what W. E. B. Du Bois would call "the talented tenth."

It has taken nearly two centuries for schoolchildren, the public, and, in fact, historians to begin learning about African Americans' revolutionary experience, a corrective to historical amnesia that is far from complete. Not that a handful of historians didn't try. Boston's William C. Nell was the first, and we should honor his efforts in the 1850s as the first chronicler of black revolutionary service. Though Nell won honors at the city's black school, white school authorities refused to include him in ceremonies bestowing laurels on Boston's outstanding young scholars. Nell turned smoldering resentment into militant abolitionism, fighting to integrate the city's public schools and contributing to William Lloyd Garrison's strident *The Liberator*. At age thirty-five Nell published a pamphlet entitled *The Services of Colored Americans in the Wars of 1776 and 1812;* he soon expanded it into a fuller *Colored Patriots of the American Revolution*. With endorsements from Harriet Beecher Stowe and Boston's Wendell Phillips, who hoped the book would "redeem the character of the [Negro] race" and "stem the tide of prejudice against the colored race," the book reached the public in 1855 just as the newspapers were reporting fearsome violence over abolitionism in "Bleeding Kansas."[1]

Working with skimpy published records, a handful

of funeral eulogies of black men who had fought in the Revolution, and oral testimonies of descendants of black patriots, Nell never hid the cards he was trying to play. Intent on showing that black men had shed their blood for the nation as freely as whites, he told dramatic stories about black heroism and sacrifice for the "glorious cause." This was an imbalanced account of the African Americans' Revolution because it ignored the huge number of men and women, mostly enslaved, who fled to and fought alongside the British in order to gain their freedom. This silence is understandable, given the rabid Negrophobia in the North that abolitionists confronted. We can imagine that Nell must have concluded that publicizing the fact that most slaves of the revolutionary era had believed that life, liberty, and happiness were best pursued with the British would cripple the abolitionists' cause.[2]

For many decades, the dirty secret that black Americans' quest for liberty was mostly tied to fighting for the British—the side in the War for Independence that offered them freedom—remained only in the memories of descendants of black participants in the war.[3] Not until 1922 did Carter G. Woodson, the second African American to receive a doctorate in history (after W. E. B. Du Bois) dare to include a para-

3

graph in *The Negro in Our History* about the thousands of Virginia, South Carolina, and Georgia slaves who had fled to the British during the war. But Woodson stepped gingerly. In his account, most African Americans, whether enslaved or free, were valorous patriotic Americans.[4]

Meanwhile, public school and college students and the public in general learned almost nothing about the African American revolutionary experience from the books that commanded library shelves—multivolume nineteenth-century histories of the United States by George Bancroft, Richard Hildreth, Edward Channing, and Henry Adams; twentieth-century schoolbooks from the pens of Woodrow Wilson, Charles Francis Adams, Charles and Mary Beard, David Mussey, and others. In these tomes, the treatment of black history in general is so paltry that it would appear that the British and the Americans fought for seven years as if half a million African Americans had been magically whisked off the continent. For any historian who bothered to mention people of African descent, as Harvard's John Fiske did, a few sentences sufficed. "The relations between master and slave in Virginia," wrote Fiske, "were so pleasant that the offer of freedom [from the British] fell upon dull, uninterested ears. With light work and generous fare, the condition of the Virginia negro was a happy one . . . He was proud of his connection with his master's estate and family, and had nothing to gain by rebellion."[5]

Only in 1940 would a slim pamphlet set the stage for turning upside down the historical understanding of black revolutionary involvement. In *The Negro in the American Revolution,* Herbert Aptheker, steeled by the American Communist Party's recruitment and defense of black Americans, tried to shatter the peculiar combination of white indifference to black history and strategic black myopia. Aptheker began with the pragmatic notion that the Revolution offered black people, most of whom were enslaved, options never before available in their quest for freedom—a freedom they understood not through political philosophy or political interests but simply as an escape from lifelong, heritable slavery. He did not ignore African Americans who served in the American army and navy, providing for the first time an estimate of about five thousand such men. But against that number, Aptheker reckoned some hundred thousand blacks who fled their masters to join the British after Lord Dunmore, Virginia's royal governor, issued his earth-shaking proclamation in late 1775 offering freedom to any slave or indentured servant who joined the British with a willingness to fight against the treasonous Americans. The cat was now out of the bag: massive defection from slavery among a people pictured by white historians as docile and contented. African Americans, wrote Aptheker, "played what at first glance appears to have been a dual role from 1775 to 1783"—service with American forces "when they were permitted to do so" and wholesale flight to the British in search of freedom. These "varied and superficially contradictory activities" had "one common origin, one set purpose—the achievement of liberty." As in every epoch of African American history, he reasoned, "the desire for freedom is the central theme, the motivating force."[6]

In 1961 Benjamin Quarles employed Aptheker's new conceptual framework to produce his classic *The Negro in the American Revolution*. In the book's preface, Quarles stated: "The Negro's role in the Revolution can best be understood by realizing that his major loyalty was not to a place nor to a people but to a principle. Insofar as he had freedom of choice, he was likely to join the side that made him the quickest and best offer in terms of those 'unalienable rights' of which Mr. Jefferson had spoken." A sprawling scholarship since 1961, detailed in scores of entries that tumble off the pages of *The Harvard Guide to African-American History* (2001), proceeds from Quarles's remarkable achievement.

In this chapter I explore the varieties of black revolutionary experience, with vignettes of individual men and women who can stand for large numbers of others. In the whole, it is a story of an extraordinary willingness—some would call it recklessness—to seize the moment to secure what was prized above all else: freedom. White revolutionaries talked about taking "a leap into the dark," by which they meant a courageous venture against seemingly insurmountable odds as they pitted a desire for independence against a tyranny-minded, overpowering English government. For African Americans, the leap into the dark was even bolder, so outlandish in its presumption that the distant shore of freedom could be reached that we can only marvel after more than two hundred years that men and women of dark skin even tried.

Barzillai Lew was typical of the free black patriot under arms, the kind of man Nell featured in his books. Tall and strong, a man with great musical talent, Lew was born free in 1743 and grew up in Dracut, Massachusetts. In 1760, at age seventeen, he served in the Seven Years' War. Three weeks after the firefights at Concord and Lexington in April 1775, he enlisted in the Massachusetts 27th Regiment, a unit forming in Chelmsford, where he was living with his wife and four children, the youngest born ten days after the shot heard round the world. Lew was one of some one hundred fifty African Americans who fought at Bunker Hill, making up about five percent of the patriots there. He reenlisted a month later to march to Fort Ticonderoga, where his unit served under the leadership of Benedict Arnold in an epic battle. He reenlisted again in late 1777. Eventually the father of thirteen children, he lived to age seventy-eight, dying in 1822.[7]

Lew embodied the "spirit of '76." White men of his age and family responsibilities enlisted en masse in the early days of the war, when the *rage militaire* animated almost all New Englanders. But few white patriots reenlisted twice more. At the Battle of Bunker Hill, and later in the Battle of Rhode Island, black soldiers from the northern states served in twice the proportion of their number in the population. The best estimates of their service indicate that throughout the entire course of the war they responded to the call to arms more readily than white men.[8]

One reason for this was that after the first flush of patriotism the Revolution turned into a poor man's

Agrippa Hull. Unknown artist, after daguerrotype by Anson
Clark. Stockbridge Library Association Historical Collection,
Stockbridge, MA.

One of the free black men who enlisted in the Continental Army
was Agrippa Hull of Stockbridge, Massachusetts. Assigned as an
orderly to General William Paterson, and then to the Polish
military engineer Thaddeus Kosciuszko, Hull served for six years
in the struggle for American independence. Kosciuszko never
forgot Hull and arranged to see him when he returned to the
United States in 1797. Hull lived out his life in Stockbridge,
where he was a living legend of the revolutionary days, a
raconteur in demand at weddings and other social gatherings.
The painting's artist is a mystery to this day, though it is
possible that Joseph Whiting Stock, a local artist, is the one
who captured Hull at about eighty-eight years of age.

war. Since most black New Englanders were poor, they became targets for recruiting sergeants. Also relevant was that some black men enlisted to gain their freedom as well as to serve the cause of independence. Peter Salem of Framingham, Massachusetts, who fired the shot that killed Major John Pitcairn, in charge of the redcoated British at Bunker Hill, signed up with his master's pledge to grant his freedom. Salem's story was that of thousands of African Americans and white indentured servants in the North, who gambled they would survive their enlistment and enter civilian life as free men. Mostly young, they embarked on a double quest for freedom: independence for America and personal independence. A Hessian officer, fighting for the British, observed in 1777: "The Negro can take the field instead of his master; and, therefore, no regiment is seen in which there are not negroes in abundance, and among them are able-bodied, strong and brave fellows."[9]

Early in the war, black Americans had to fight for the right to fight. New Englanders at first were glad to have men of color fighting alongside them. (It needs remembering that this would be the last war with integrated troops until the Korean War nearly two centuries later.) But pressure from white southern leaders led General Washington to purge his army of African Americans with an order issued on November 12, 1775, just five days after Virginia's royal governor offered freedom to slaves who reached his encampment. Within six weeks, already fearful that he would be unable to maintain a large fighting force, Washington partially reversed his order. With congressional approval, he reopened the Continental Army to free black men, though not to slaves.

In the Valley Forge winter of 1778–79 Washington further amended his recruitment policy. Struggling to regroup his manpower-starved army, he accepted a proposal to raise a regiment of slaves from Rhode Island. The state's legislature used lofty language to endorse the idea: "History affords us frequent precedents of the wisest, the freest, and bravest nations having liberated their slaves and enlisted them as soldiers to fight in defense of their country." On the ground, the motives were less lofty. The historian Lorenzo Greene is surely right in arguing that the proposal was "inspired by stark necessity." Like other states, Rhode Island by this time was reaching for the bottom of the social barrel to recruit poor white men for regiments thinned by disease, absenteeism, and outright desertion. White Rhode Islanders now rebuilt what some called "the ragged lousey naked regiment" with slaves liberated by their masters, who were promised compensation from the public coffers for their loss of labor.[10]

That liberated slaves might tip the balance for the beleaguered forces under Washington's command became a distinct possibility in March 1779. In one of its boldest steps of the entire war, one that had the promise of riveting together the war for independence with the efforts to reform America, the Continental Congress urged Georgia and South Carolina to recruit three thousand stoutly built slaves to help repulse the British forces pillaging and plundering their way through Georgia and into South Carolina. Though the slaves themselves would receive no pay, their masters would get compensation for the loss of property, and each slave who survived the war would have his freedom and fifty dollars to begin life anew.[11]

Eager to oversee the recruitment of slaves was twenty-five-year-old John Laurens, scion of one of South Carolina's wealthiest and most politically potent families, aide-de-camp to Washington, and a reformer who dreamed that American independence would bring liberty to half a million slaves as well. Laurens had seen black men fight bravely in the battle of Newport eight months before, where he had led a contingent almost alongside the mostly black Rhode Island First Regiment. Laurens argued that bolstering the faltering American army with slaves would reward "those who are unjustly deprived of the rights of mankind." Alexander Hamilton and many others in Washington's military circle endorsed the plan, and other leading South Carolinians, including Laurens's father, William Drayton, and Daniel Huger, supported the idea as the only way South Carolina could defend itself against the massed British attackers. But the general himself, fearing that enlisting slaves would "render slavery more irksome to those who remain in it," withheld his support. Washington's backing of the plan might possibly have convinced South Carolina's and Georgia's planter-politicians to accept it, which would have changed the entire character of the American Revolution. The fear of seeing enslaved men under arms was no doubt palpable. Congress's proposal, huffed Christopher Gadsden of South Carolina, "was received with great resentment as a very dangerous and impolitic step."[12] South Carolinians responded in this manner in the absence of Washington's support; it can be only a matter of speculation whether Washington's enormous prestige might have convinced slaveowners of the Lower South that it would be better to free some of their slaves to fight *against* the British invaders than to see them flee *to* the British.

Fighting in American regiments offered one avenue out of a lifetime in slavery for able-bodied men in
the North, though this was a case-by-case struggle
for black freedom. A much smaller number of black
northerners understood that they might use the war
as a lever to end slavery altogether. Never before in
the history of North American enslavement had they
held at their disposal the words of white colonists
that could be potent weapons in their fight for freedom. White defenses of "natural rights" in protests
against English policies, and street and tavern talk
about the "immutable laws of nature" and the legiti-
macy of defying tyranny, were like so much cognitive
shrapnel exploding in the kitchens, stables, barns,

---

Emanuel Leutze, *Washington Crossing the Delaware,* 1850. The
Metropolitan Museum of Art, Gift of John S. Kennedy, 1897
(97.34).

In this famous painting, the stroke oar in the bow is held by
Prince Whipple—or so he is identified by William C. Nell,
Boston's historian of "the colored patriots" of the American
Revolution, in a book published just after Leutze's painting
attracted fifty thousand people in New York, where it was first
exhibited. African-born Prince Whipple was the bodyguard of
New Hampshire's General William Whipple, one of
Washington's aides.

fields, and docksides where slaves toiled from morning to night. The more such rhetoric entered public discourse, the more enslaved African Americans saw an opportunity to expose the glaring anomaly of freedom-loving patriots embracing slavery. Indeed, by the mid-1760s, with white leaders saying as much, the idea of birthright freedom lodged unshakably in black minds.

Boston provides a vivid example. Enslaved men and women there could hardly have overlooked James Otis's frontal assault on slavery in 1764, when, while defending American colonists against invasion of their rights by their British overlords, he asserted: "The colonists are by the law of nature free born, as indeed all men are, white or black . . . Does it follow that 'tis right to enslave a man because he is black? Will short curled hair . . . instead of Christian hair, as 'tis called by those whose hearts are as hard as the nether millstone, help the argument? Can any logical inference in favour of slavery be drawn from a flat nose, a long or a short face?"[13]

Far to the south in Virginia, slaves similarly could hardly have missed the assertion of Arthur Lee, published in the most widely read newspaper in the southern colonies in 1767, that "freedom is unquestionably the birth-right of all mankind, of Africans

as well as Europeans" and that slavery "is in violation of justice and religion." That change was in the
air up and down the seaboard was evident for all to
see. Boston's town meeting soon pushed for a law
to ban further importation and sale of slaves, and
by 1773 Harvard honors students were devoting the
commencement debate to the morality and legality
of slavery. As Bernard Bailyn puts it: "The identifica-
tion between the cause of the colonies and the cause
of the Negroes bound in chattel slavery—an identi-
fication built into the very language of politics—
became inescapable."[14]

We can only imagine how word of mounting in-
dictments of slavery must have struck the tens of
thousands of enslaved Africans in the North: it must
have seemed that perpetually dark clouds had
opened to allow bright rays of sun to shine. But
should they wait for white legislators and individual slave owners to end their travails? Most were lead-
erless and isolated, unable to do more than hope and
wait. But some pursued one of two strategies: su-
ing their masters individually to gain freedom or
petitioning legislatures to abolish slavery altogether.
Jenny Slew of Salem, Massachusetts, was one of the
former. Plucking up her courage, she went to a local
court with an appeal to restore what she claimed was

her birthright freedom. John Adams witnessed Slew win her case and told his diary that he had "heard there have been many" such cases. Years later, he remembered: "I never know a jury by a verdict to determine a negro to be a slave. They always found him free."[15] Freedom suits now multiplied in the courts of small country towns dotting the New England landscape, where nonslaveholders composed most juries. But in Boston, where many jurors owned slaves, the better strategy for slaves was to petition the legislature for a general emancipation.

This happened three and a half years before the Declaration of Independence. In the first week of 1773, "many Slaves, living in the Town of Boston and other towns in the province," submitted the first petition found by historians asking for a general release from slavery. Enslaved residents of Massachusetts had taken a page from the patriots' book of tactics, organizing themselves to speak as one from many towns—a kind of informal committee of correspondence. The petition sorrowfully described slaves "who have had every day of their lives embittered with this most intolerable reflection, that, let their behaviour be what it will, nor their children to all generations, shall ever be able to do, or to possess and enjoy anything, no not even *life itself*, but in a manner as the *beasts that perish.*"[16] The black protest, mixing humility with striking self-assertion, assumed the character of a broadside to be nailed to tavern doors, lampposts, and other public places. Within weeks an anonymous friend of the slaves published the petition as a small pamphlet with two letters appended, one by "A Lover of True Liberty," the other by "The Sons of Africa."

The petition did not succeed, but neither was it a failure, for it spurred a debate in the legislature over abolishing slavery. Three months later, again borrowing from the white patriot strategy book, four black men published a hard-hitting leaflet in which they spoke for "our fellow slaves in this province." They began tauntingly: "We expect great things from men who have made such a noble stand against the designs of their *fellow-men* to enslave them"—a clear reference to British policies that colonists regarded as tantamount to stripping away their freedoms. The petition went on with a passage that showed that word of the Spanish practice of *coartación*—the legal right of Spanish slaves to buy their way out of slavery—had spread to New England. "Even the Spaniards," the petitioners pointed out, "who have not those sublime ideas of freedom that English men have, are conscious that they have no right to all the services of their fellow-men, we mean the Africans . . . ; therefore they allow them one day a week to work for themselves, to enable them to earn money to purchase the residue of their time, which they have a right to demand in such portions as they are able to pay for."[17]

Disappointed by legislative inaction on the issue of slavery, black activists tried again in 1774 with more strenuous language: "A great number of blacks of the Province . . . held in a state of slavery within the bowels of a free and Christian country, have . . . in common with all other men a natural right to our freedoms . . . as we are a freeborn people and have never forfeited this blessing by any compact or agreement whatever."[18] This time the legislature partly answered the petition by passing a law banning further importation of enslaved Africans, only to have Governor Thomas Hutchinson, whose friends included slave importers, veto it. Yet the black petitioners made slavery a major topic of discussion, bringing thousands of the enslaved to a state of anticipation.

Freedom suits and petitions finally paid off in Massachusetts thanks to a woman who was all humbleness on the surface but iron underneath. Mum Bett grew up enslaved in Sheffield, in western Massachusetts, where she heard her share of the white townsmen's rhetoric in their struggle against British oppression. Her owner fought briefly in the war, and her husband fell on a Massachusetts battlefield. She may have followed the heated debates over a constitution for Massachusetts and known that many towns wanted the abolition of slavery written into the state's constitution. But the constitution that belatedly emerged in 1780 was silent on slavery, although the language of its declaration of rights would later be used to argue that slavery was impermissible.

A year later an incident of a sort common between enslavers and enslaved brought matters to a head. Amidst a fierce argument, Mum Bett threw herself between her sister and their angry white mistress, who struck at her with a heated fire shovel. Mum Bett received the blow on her arm, "the scar of which she bore to the day of her death." Outraged, she stalked from the house and refused to return. When her master appealed to the local court to recover his slave, Mum Bett called upon a lawyer from nearby Stockbridge to ask if the new Massachusetts constitution, with its preamble stating that "all men are born free and equal," did not apply to her. Theodore Sedgwick took the case and argued that Mum Bett was "entitled to the same privileges as other human beings" whose skin was pigmented differently. When the jury agreed, Mum Bett walked away a free woman and shortly renamed herself Elizabeth Freeman to mark this milestone in her life.

The case set a precedent. The state's highest court upheld it two years later with striking words that ended a century and a half of slavery in Massachusetts: "Is not a law of nature that all men are equal and free? Is not the laws of nature the laws of God? Is not the law of God then against slavery?"[19] A household slave had become an agent of change in New England's most populous state. Catharine Maria Sedgwick, the daughter of the man who took Mum Bett's suit to court, remembered many years later that his client would say emphatically: "Any time while I was a slave, if one minute's freedom had been offered to me, and I had been told I must die at the end of that minute, I would have taken it just to stand one minute on God's airth a free woman, I would."[20]

Many enslaved people could not wait for benevolent owners to set them free, wait for legislatures or courts to declare slavery unconstitutional, or hope their master would send them to serve in the army in his place. An unprecedented alternative was now available—flight from slavery to the sheltering arms of an occupying army. Fleeing slavery had always been an option, utilized by a few percent of enslaved men every year and perhaps half as many women. But that was flight *from* slavery with the hope of posing successfully as free men or women. Now, for the first time in generations of captivity, there was a chance to flee *toward* a force prepared to guarantee freedom to the slave on the run. Before, this had been possible only for handfuls of slaves who fled southward from South Carolina and Georgia over miles of unknown terrain to seek sanctuary in Spanish Florida.[21] Now a place of refuge was as close as the British army.

This triggered the greatest slave rebellion in North American history—one almost too shocking for the American public to contemplate even now. Media moguls think so, it seems. For example, Hollywood's film *The Patriot* (2001) gets it right when Benjamin Martin, the British officer, gallops onto a South Carolina plantation and offers freedom to any slaves ready to fight with the British, the first time in film history that such an idea has hit the silver screen. But then the movie stands history on its head. The supposed slaves declare that they are free black workers who happily work for wages paid by a caring white plantation owner. There can be no slave rebellion on this plantation—the only one the movie viewers see—

because there are no slaves. Hollywood murders history again when Occam, a northern slave, sees a proclamation from General Washington and the Continental Congress offering freedom in return for one year of a slave's military service. But it was the British army, not the American army, that issued an emancipation proclamation.

The history of British emancipatory policy is still murky. The current understanding is that the British decided in late 1775, after deliberating policy choices hinging on military strategy, to offer freedom to slaves fleeing their masters; then the slaves responded. But the reverse may be truer. Fourteen months before Lord Dunmore's famous proclamation of November 1775, enslaved Bostonians offered to take up the sword against their masters. The town was crawling with British soldiers, of the 14th and 29th Regiments, and Governor Thomas Gage had dissolved the Massachusetts legislature, thereby foreclosing that avenue of ending slavery. Now slaves moved from imploring words to self-assertion. "There has been in town a conspiracy of the Negroes," Abigail Adams wrote to her husband, who was in Philadelphia as a delegate to the First Continental Congress. "At present, it is kept pretty private and was discovered by one who endeavored to dissuade them from it." The slaves, Abigail continued, threatened the life of the man who might reveal their plot, and proceeded "to draw up a petition to the Governor, telling him they would fight for him provided he would arm them and engage to liberate them if he conquered." For white Bostonians, priding themselves on being a different breed from southern slave masters, this came as a shock. Benjamin Franklin's judgment of nearly twenty years before, that "every slave may be reckoned a domestic enemy," was chillingly confirmed. Seven months later, in Rhode Island, the northern center of Atlantic slave trading, slaves slipped away with a group of thirty-five white loyalists who had obtained arms from a British man-of-war stationed in Newport.[22]

Enslaved Virginians were not far behind New England slaves in helping to shape British policy rather than simply responding to it. In eastern Virginia, reported the young James Madison, some of them met in November 1774 to choose a leader, "who was to conduct them when the English troops should arrive." Madison believed the slaves "foolishly thought . . . that by revolting to [the British] they should be rewarded with their freedom." But he soon learned that the slaves were not foolish at all but were anticipating and promoting what soon became British policy. In early 1775 slaves in tidewater Virginia staged a rash of uprisings, pushing Virginia's governor to capitalize on their boldness. On April 21, only two days after the minutemen riddled Gage's troops sent to capture the colonial arsenals at Lexington and Concord, determined slaves in Williamsburg slipped word to Dunmore that they were ready to flee their masters, join him, and "take up arms." Ten days later Dunmore wrote to the secretary of state in London setting out his plan "to arm all my own Negroes, and receive all others that will come to me whom I shall declare free." The shot heard 'round the world at Concord Bridge was the white people's shot; for half a million black people, the shot heard through slave cabins came six months later when Dunmore's decision, approved in London, was officially enunciated.[23]

Among the first to flee to Dunmore were eight of the twenty-seven slaves who toiled at the stately Williamsburg dwelling of Peyton Randolph, the speaker of Virginia's House of Burgesses and one of Virginia's delegates to the Continental Congress, of which he would serve as president for several months. Three of the eight were women. Visitors to Colonial Williamsburg today learn their names and see them pictured as freedom fighters rather than faithless slaves—part of Colonial Williamsburg's transformed presentation of the past. Eluding slave patrols, Randolph's slaves reached the British forces not far from town. Three weeks later Lund Washington, manager of his cousin's Mount Vernon estate, warned that among the slaves and indentured servants "there is not a man of them but would leave us, if they could make their escape." He captured the mass defection under way in three words: "Liberty is sweet."[24]

It was shocking to slaveowners that slaves fled in groups because they were accustomed only to individual slaves, or perhaps two or three at a time, escaping to find relatives or friends. But even more shocking was that many enslaved women made a dash for freedom. For many years only about one-eighth of slave runaways had been female, not surprising since most women had young children, were pregnant, or were otherwise tied to family. But the flight of Randolph's slaves prefigured the pattern that would prevail over the next seven years: about one-third of all those claiming liberty under flight to the British were women. In one list of eighty-seven slaves who fled to Dunmore, twenty-one were women, twenty-three were girls under age sixteen, sixteen were men, and twenty-seven were boys under sixteen. Many of them fled as families, with one slave as old as sixty and half a dozen only babes in arms.[25] Some eight hundred to a thousand fled to Dunmore and hundreds more fell into the hands of patrolling patriots while trying to do so. The slaves of many of Virginia's leading white revolutionary figures had now become black revolutionary Virginians themselves—a development that "raised our country into perfect frenzy," according to Jefferson.[26]

Dunmore formed the men into the British Ethiopian Regiment and outfitted some of them with white sashes bearing the inscription "Liberty to Slaves." Commanding the Ethiopian Regiment was the British officer Thomas Byrd, the son of the American patriot William Byrd III, whose name symbolized Virginia wealth in land and slaves. The Ethiopian Regiment fought "with the intrepidity of lions," according to one American who faced them at Great Bridge south of Norfolk less than a month after Dunmore's Proclamation.[27]

Having retreated from Williamsburg to Norfolk with his Ethiopian and British regiments, Dunmore then boarded warships anchored in Chesapeake Bay, from which his men forayed out to seize provisions from waterside plantations. Reaching Dunmore's forces now became more difficult because fleeing slaves had to commandeer watercraft and slip down to the bay in hopes of clambering aboard British ships. Many took the chance. But stalking these bold attempts at self-liberation was a killer even more dangerous than the white slave patrols. Sweeping eastern North America in 1775–76, smallpox spread rapidly through the crowded British ships and on Gwynn's Island in Chesapeake Bay, which Dunmore briefly occupied in the summer of 1776. Dunmore admitted that smallpox "carried off an incredible number of our people, especially blacks."[28] By July 1776, as Congress was declaring independence, he withdrew his disease-riddled forces, sending part of them to St. Augustine, Florida, and the Bermudas; others, including three hundred of the strongest and healthiest black soldiers, went by ship to New York City and would later return southward for a land assault through Maryland to Pennsylvania that climaxed with the British occupation of Philadelphia in September 1777.

Pennsylvania slaveowners feared the conquering British army that invaded the state in the autumn of 1777, but they had few fears that their slaves would defect to the British because they imagined themselves as humane masters and had witnessed not a single slave uprising over nearly a century. They were wrong. After the British mauled the Americans at

Brandywine, with several hundred Black Guides and Pioneers in train, they promptly occupied Philadelphia. Far from remaining faithful to their masters, the slaves, confided the Lutheran minister Henry Muhlenberg to his diary, "secretly wished that the British army might win, for then all Negro slaves will gain their freedom," a belief that "is almost universal among the Negroes in America." The flight of hundreds of slaves in the Philadelphia region to the British during the nine-month occupation of the Quaker city confirmed Muhlenberg's insight that relatively humane treatment provided little insurance against slave flight. Looking back after the British evacuated the city in the summer of 1778, one Philadelphian wrote that "the defection [to the British] of the Negroes of the most indulgent masters . . . shewed what little dependence ought to be placed on persons deprived of their natural liberty."[29]

The flight to the British army in the early years of the war, as much as it shocked slaveowners in both northern and southern states, was only the first wave of what became a massive self-emancipation by the South's enslaved population after the war stalemated in the North in 1779. Returning in force to the South, where a black fifth column could provide a decisive edge, the British struck to conquer. In what must be accounted as the greatest slave rebellion in the history of Great Britain's New World colonies, black men, women, and children flocked to the invading British army. No doubt they remembered that relatives and friends had died like diseased sheep when smallpox tore through Dunmore's Chesapeake military encampments in 1776. They knew also that white slaveowners had dealt harshly with the kinfolk of those who had deserted to the British. Not knowing what awaited them if they reached the British lines must also have gnawed at the resolve of many. Yet large numbers took their chances, willing to die free, even if after only a day, a week, or a month of freedom, rather than remain enslaved for life.

British strategists selected Georgia, which was brimming with Americans loyal to the Crown, as the base from which the southern states could be severed from the North. If this was successful, they believed, American resistance would crumble. Attacking by land and sea from East Florida in 1779, the British required only a month to gain control of Georgia. For some fifteen thousand Georgia slaves, this victory afforded only limited chances for gaining their liberty, because most of them were owned by white loyalists. This was human property that the British could not afford to touch. Slaves owned by white patriots had a better chance, but when white patriots fled the state in nearly a mass exodus, they took most of their slaves with them. The American officer William Moultrie witnessed "the poor women and children, and negroes of Georgia, many thousands of whom I saw, . . . traveling to they knew not where."[30]

We know little about whether word of Laurens's unsuccessful proposal to free slaves to bolster the American army reached the ears of southern slaves, though it is unlikely that the news could have been kept from them. We do know that slaves in Virginia understood that their prospects for freedom changed radically when British schooners and barges began maneuvering up the rivers flowing into the Chesapeake in November 1780. This was the opportunity enslaved Virginians had been awaiting since Governor Dunmore had fled Williamsburg four years before. Back then, only slaves in a limited geographical area had been able to reach his forces. But now British forces rampaged far into the Virginia interior, opening the way for massive slave defections. As the British swept ashore to burn houses and barns, "slaves flock[ed] to them from every quarter," reported a local planter. In January 1781, when Benedict Arnold's squadron of sixteen hundred men stormed up the James River to Richmond to plunder the region, James Madison's father wrote to him: "Families within the sphere of his action have suffered greatly. Some have lost 40 [slaves], others 30, and one a considerable part of their slaves." In March, after Arnold continued his forays into the James River area, doctor Robert Honyman reported that slaves "flocked to the enemy from all quarters, even from very remote parts." Many planters lost from thirty to seventy slaves.[31]

British raids up the Potomac River in April 1781 brought new opportunities for Virginia slaves. Robert Carter, one of the area's premier planters, lost thirty-two of his slaves when the British sloop *Savage* landed at his Cole's Point plantation. At Washington's Mount Vernon, the sloop carried off fourteen men and three women. Almost defenseless against this onslaught, hundreds of tidewater planters loaded wagons with their most valuable possessions and headed for the interior with slaves in tow. In early June 1781, General Charles Cornwallis took special delight in making his headquarters at Jefferson's Elk Hill plantation in Goochland County, where for ten days Cornwallis's troops, accompanied by escaped slaves, destroyed barns and rustled cattle, sheep, hogs, and horses. When they left, Black Sall, three of her children, and seven other Jefferson slaves joined the British, while another eight fled his Cumberland

County plantation. When Cornwallis dispatched Banastre Tarleton's dragoons to capture Jefferson and members of the Virginia legislature who had retreated to Charlottesville, Virginia's governor escaped with his family, but four of his Monticello slaves decamped with the British. Richard Henry Lee counted the loss of slaves on other plantations: forty-five from the plantation of his brother William Lee, all of the slaves of Edward Taliaferro and Edward Travis, and all but one slave of Richard Paradise. Thomas Nelson, governor of Virginia, lost all but eighty to a hundred of his seven hundred slaves, according to a German officer who served with French troops. "This has been the general case of all those who were near the enemy," Lee wrote to his brother in July 1781. The Hessian officer Johann Ewald believed that "well over four thousand Negroes of both sexes and all ages" were now part of Cornwallis's British army.[32]

Virginia's stricken plantation owners liked to think that the British had compelled their slaves to abandon them. "Whenever they had an opportunity," noted Robert Honyman, "the soldiers and inferior officers likewise, enticed and flattered the Negroes and prevailed on vast numbers to go along with them." Richard Henry Lee was indignant that "force, fraud, intrigue, theft, have all in turn been employed to delude these unhappy people and to defraud their masters!" Was this the case? Probably not, because when Cornwallis's army approached, slaves could have fled *from* rather than *toward* the British. To be sure, many slaves acted "under the combined weight of prudence, caution, fear, and realism," as Sylvia Frey puts it, and therefore remained with their masters as the British approached.[33] But those who struck out for freedom in the face of heavy odds were hardly "deluded," as Richard Henry Lee believed. And most would have laughed at the notion that they were "defrauding" their masters. Slaves by the thousands had waited for years for the British army to heave into sight. Believing this was their last best chance, thousands demonstrated an unquenchable thirst for freedom by fleeing to the British on the eve of the momentous military climax at Yorktown.

A particularly vivid account, scribbled in the diary of a Hessian officer, gives insight into how the most intrepid slaves, both women and men, exacted their pound of flesh from their former masters. Johann Ewald, thousands of miles from his home in Germany, described escaped slaves who, after reaching British camps, joined foraging parties to plunder the wardrobes of their masters and mistresses. With relish, they "divided the loot, and clothed themselves piecemeal with it . . . A completely naked Negro wore a pair of silk breeches, another a finely colored coat, a third a silk vest without sleeves, a fourth an elegant shirt, a fifth a fine churchman's hat, and a sixth a wig.—All the rest of the body was bare!" Here was a demonstration of primitive justice. "The one Negress wore a silk skirt, another a lounging robe with a long train, the third a jacket, the fourth a silk-laced bodice, the fifth a silk corset, the seventh, eighth, and ninth—all different styles of hats and coiffures." The overall tableau amazed Colonel Ewald: "These variegated creatures on thousands of horses" trailing behind the British army baggage train reminded him of "a wandering Arabian or Tarter horde."[34] For slaves who for years had had little but skimpy and worn clothing, here was one of freedom's rewards, momentary to be sure but nonetheless sweet.

But the gamble for freedom in the heart of the Virginia slaveocracy was almost at an end. Decamping from Richmond and moving down the James River, Cornwallis's army reached Williamsburg on June 25, 1781. After occupying the town for ten days, the British general moved his army on to Jamestown and then in August to the small tobacco port of Yorktown. Formed into shovel brigades, several thousand black refugees built stout fortifications for Cornwallis's seven thousand troops, who were preparing to do battle with the French naval force moving into the Chesapeake Bay and the American land forces gathering to lay siege. Meanwhile, even before they reached Yorktown, hundreds of escaped slaves were struck down by a terrifying outbreak of smallpox. "Within these days past, I have marched by 18 or 20 Negroes that lay dead by the way-side, putrifying with the small pox," noted a Connecticut soldier.[35] Others, similarly infected, limped on to Yorktown.

In the siege that began on September 28, 1781, hunger became Cornwallis's biggest problem but disease was not far behind. When forage for animals ran out, Cornwallis ordered hundreds of horses slaughtered and thrown into the York River. Then, with rations dwindling for his troops, he expelled thousands of black auxiliaries from his encampments. Colonel Johann Ewald found this shameful: "We had used them to good advantage and set them free, and now, with fear and trembling, they had to face the reward of their cruel masters." Ewald encountered "a great number of these unfortunates" half-starved and hiding in the woods.[36] But Cornwallis was not so merciless as it appears. With surrender imminent, every black man and woman was a hair's breadth away from certain return to slavery. Forced out of the British fortifications, the black refugees at least had a chance of escaping. General Charles O'Hara, a senior officer in Cornwallis's army, remembered leaving four hundred black refugees with provisions to get them through smallpox and placing them in "the most friendly quarter in our neighborhood," where he begged "local residents to be kind to the refugees he had once sheltered."[37]

When the Americans and French entered Yorktown on October 19, 1781, they found "an immense number of Negroes" lying dead "in the most miserable manner" from smallpox. Within days of the British surrender, planters descended on Yorktown and began hiring pay-starved American soldiers to ferret surviving ex-slaves out of the woods. Private Joseph Martin was among those who accepted a guinea (twenty-one shillings) per head for those he rounded up. Writing of his wartime experiences much later, he remembered that some of the American soldiers would not hand over the former slaves of John Banister, a Virginia planter and legislator, "unless he would promise not to punish them."[38]

Thus ended the greatest tragedy of the American Revolution for African Americans. Those expelled from the British fortifications at Yorktown had little chance for escape, and even that chance was severely minimized by the smallpox epidemic that stalked Cornwallis's march eastward from Richmond to Yorktown. Seven years later Jefferson estimated that about twenty-seven thousand of some thirty thousand Virginia slaves who fled to the British had died of smallpox and camp fevers. Historians have argued recently that Jefferson greatly exaggerated the number of absconding Virginia slaves. Current research suggests one-third that many.[39] But the patriarch of Monticello was right about the horrendous effect of the smallpox. The fate of his own escaped slaves was probably typical. Of the thirty who fled to the British, at least fifteen died from typhus and smallpox. He recovered six others after the Yorktown surrender and sold or gave away most of them within a few years.[40] The others escaped and were lost to him—and to history. The British southern campaign, meant to bring the Americans to their knees, marked the height of the greatest slave rebellion in American history. Despite their determination to make themselves free, disease and the outcome of the Yorktown siege put most of the black refugees in shallow graves after only the briefest taste of half-freedom.

The minority of escaping slaves who survived the war, perhaps only one of every six, faced great uncertainty as the war wound down. American diplomats put intense pressure on the British to return all American slaves to their former owners, but this the British refused to do. That left the question of where they would take some ten thousand black British subjects. When the British fleet hove into sight in Savannah in the spring of 1782 to evacuate the British army and loyalist supporters, the decision was thrust upon the British. Georgia's legislature urgently petitioned the English commander to allow planters to cross British lines and claim their former slaves. The commander refused, leaving the Americans to deplore the way the Crown officials "hurried away with our Negroes."[41] About four thousand African Americans sailed away in July 1782, most of them as slaves of departing Georgia loyalists. With British shipping inadequate to carry them all, some slaves went with their masters on small private ships, others in small craft and even canoes for a water passage southward along the coast to British Florida.

As the British completed the Savannah evacuation, other Crown officials prepared to repeat the process in Charleston. In the summer of 1782 they awaited the decision of the American and British commissioners, who had argued for months over the question of fugitive slaves. The Americans' best card in this diplomacy was the threat to repudiate debts owed to British merchants before the Revolution. On the other hand, the British could return the refugees for American promises not to confiscate the property of South Carolina loyalists. In the end, officials in London decided not to surrender any refugee slave who had been explicitly promised freedom or any whose military service for the British might lead to ugly reprisals by former masters. For these ex-slaves, the British promised full compensation to former owners.

The scene that ensued was surely rare, perhaps unprecedented, in history. The only way to decide whether a man or woman had been promised freedom or legitimately feared reprisal if returned to his or her master was the African American's own testimony. Thus, by agreement, a committee of loyalist civilians and British officers met at the statehouse in early November 1782 to listen to the refugees' stories. Waiting in line by the hundreds to give their accounts, many freed people were cajoled by former masters to return to their plantations. But inducing those who had tasted freedom to refasten their chains was, by definition, an absurdity. One planter "used every argument I was master of to get them to return, but to no effect," and "several of them . . . told me with an air of insolence they were not going back." South Carolina planters were sure that sympathetic British members of the committee coached the refugees so their stories would be convincing. But what slave needed to be told what to say? Major General Alexander Leslie was staggered by the number who came forward to plead for freedom. "From the numbers that may expect to be brought off," he wrote to Carleton, "including their wives and children, if to be paid for will amount to a monstrous expense." In disgust, as the British officers accepted the black refugees' stories, the loyalist Americans resigned from the committee. John Rutledge, former South Carolina governor, believed that the commissioners ruled in favor of "almost every Negro, man, woman, and child, that was worth the carrying away."[42]

For the slaves still in the grasp of loyalists poised to leave South Carolina, the problem was different. To stay off the departing ships, not on them, was their only hope for freedom, because almost the entire British flotilla was sailing for the West Indies slave colonies, where sugar planters practiced the cruel institution at its worst. "Secreted away by her friends," wrote one loyalist master, his enslaved woman "got out of the way of the evacuation and remain[ed]" in the state. Another loyalist reported that his male slave "ran away overnight when they were to embark the next morning."[43] How many slipped away is not known, and only fragments of evidence remain to say how many of those who escaped found their way to freedom.

As the British fleet at Charleston prepared the final stages of evacuation in December 1782, white and black passengers filed onto the ships in an uneasy assemblage of white loyalists, their slaves, and free black men and women to whom the British had promised freedom. One debarkation report numbered 5,327 black evacuees out of a total of 9,127. Other reports suggest that the total number was at least 10,000 and perhaps even 12,000.[44] Far more of them were enslaved than free. In one debarkation list, only 160 African Americans were on ships headed for New York, Nova Scotia, and England, and these are the most likely to have been free. About 2,960 others sailed for Jamaica and St. Lucia in the West Indies, almost all scheduled for lifelong slavery. Those who went to East Florida, about 2,210, were also scheduled for continued bondage in a new location.[45] Many others, perhaps several thousand, had been trafficked out of Charleston in the months leading up to evacuation, often sold by British officers bent on leaving America with something to show for their troubles.

East Florida was still a wilderness when the British ships began unloading their human cargo in December 1782. Two hundred years of Spanish colonization had reduced the Indian population drastically, and Spanish settlers were still in the early stages of frontier agricultural development. The old fortress and mission town of St. Augustine was little more than a dusty collection of crude houses. Scattered in the hinterland were small assemblages of refugee slaves living off the land. Now East Florida became a major asylum for loyalists and their slaves. East Florida had joined Nova Scotia as a new frontier, pinning the British at the two extremities of the North American Atlantic seaboard. By early 1783 the evacuations of Savannah and Charleston, along with Cornwallis's surrender at Yorktown, added about eleven thousand people to the sparsely populated colony. Sixty percent of them were slaves.

Set to work cultivating rice, indigo, and corn and producing tar and turpentine from pine forests, some nine thousand slaves shortly found themselves pawns once again when England ceded East Florida to Spain in January 1783 as part of the peace negotiations ending the American war. The South Carolina and Georgia legislatures tried to prevent their removal in the hope that planters from those states could recover them. But the Spanish governor resisted, allowing the loyalist refugees in Florida to move with their slaves to Jamaica, the Bahamas, and other British West Indies sugar islands.[46] Seven years of hoping and fighting for liberty had yielded these evacuees nothing. Thousands of them perished in hurricanes and a deadly yellow fever epidemic in the late 1780s.

In the North, the other half of the British army prepared to evacuate New York City after word of the final peace treaty arrived in June 1783. Here lived the other large contingent of African Americans who had reached the British lines. But in contrast to those in Savannah and Charleston, these were almost all free men, women, and children. That did not ensure them continued freedom. The coming of peace, remembered Boston King, formerly a slave in South Carolina, "diffused universal joy among all parties, except us who had escaped from slavery and taken refuge in the English army." King and his wife had been part of the roving British forces for four years and had arrived in New York by ship. But now, in 1783, "a report prevailed at New-York, that all the slaves, in the number 2000, were to be delivered up to their masters, altho' some of them had been three or four years among the English. This dreadful rumor," he related in his autobiographical account, "filled us all with inexpressible anguish and terror, especially when we saw our old masters coming from Virginia, North-Carolina, and other parts, and seizing upon their slaves in the streets of New-York . . . For some days we lost our appetite for food, and sleep departed from our eyes."[47]

Then the British officers assured King and his brethren that the British would not surrender them to the mercy of their former owners. "Each of us received a certificate [of freedom] from the commanding officer at New-York, which dispelled our fears and filled us with joy and gratitude," King remembered. They were to be transported to Nova Scotia—a decision reached painfully by the British, who knew they could not take the black loyalists to England's slave-based Caribbean sugar islands, where planters would not tolerate a large number of free blacks and would attempt to re-enslave them.[48] England itself wanted no influx of ex-slaves, for Londoners and the white residents of other major cities already felt burdened by growing numbers of impoverished former slaves seeking public support.[49] Nor was East Florida much of an option since that too was a slave colony and in any event was being pawned to Spain. Only Nova Scotia remained, suitable because slavery had not taken root in this easternmost part of the Canadian wilderness that England had acquired from France at the end of the Seven Years' War. So in the winter of 1783 thousands of former American slaves disembarked from British ships to start life anew amidst sparsely scattered old French settlers, remnants of Indian tribes, loyalists from the American colonies, and war-weary British soldiers. To discharged British soldiers and black refugees the British government offered land, tools, and rations for three years.

The "Book of Negroes" kept by the British in New York contains the names, ages, and places where 2,775 black loyalists had toiled as slaves. Several thousand more had earlier left New York City and other northern port towns on merchant and troop ships. If smallpox and camp fevers hadn't wiped out thousands of African Americans who joined the British, the evacuation would have been much larger, probably three or four times as large. Nearly forty percent of the evacuees were females, and children made up about one-quarter of the total. They came from every region of the former colonies, with the largest numbers from Virginia and the Carolinas. Many had toiled for the "founding fathers" of the new American nation. On the voyage to Nova Scotia slaves who had belonged to Thomas Jefferson, George Washington, Patrick Henry, John Jay, and other white found-

ing fathers doubtless recounted stories of their enslavement and their escape.[50]

Of black Americans who survived the war, the vast
majority did not leave American shores but remained
to toil where most of them had been born. It fell to
them to carry on the dual struggle to end slavery and
create the social networks and institutional framework of free black life. These were the still largely un-
appreciated black founding fathers. Bernard Bailyn
has recently given us his appreciation of the "extraordinary generation" of white founding fathers—what
he calls "one of the most creative groups in modern
history." But just such terms can be used to describe
the black founders as well. It is no dishonor to Jefferson, Washington, Franklin, and Adams, who engaged
in what Bailyn calls "extraordinary flights of creative
imagination—political heresies at the time, utopian
fantasies," to insist that the same can be said of the
African American leaders who emerged from the
shadows after the smoke and din of war had sub-
sided. They, too, again to borrow Bailyn's phrases,
"found few precedents to follow, no models to imi-
tate." So, too, they "refused to be intimidated by the
received traditions; and, confident of their own integrity and creative capacities, they demanded to know
why things must be the way they are; and they had

*Kneeling Dinah,* ca. 1787. Private collection. Courtesy Luke Beckerdite, Williamsburg, VA.

On bended knee, Dinah Nevill, a mixed-race woman who had been sold by her New Jersey owner to a Virginia planter, watches imploringly as the Quaker with broad-brimmed hat pays the Virginian to free her and her two children. This was the first release from slavery obtained by the Pennsylvania Abolition Society, formed in 1775.

the imagination and energy to conceive of something closer to the grain of everyday reality and more likely to lead to human happiness."[51]

Such high praise is all the more fitting for the new nation's emerging black leaders because the black American people, who composed one-fifth of the population, had to begin the world anew with only rudimentary education and often with only the scantiest necessities of life. Black survivors of the Revolution brought to the task of starting *their* world anew an accumulation of disabilities—years of unceasing and unpaid toil, brutal treatment, efforts to keep them illiterate, cruelties that tore at their family fabric, and the disdain of most white people. Thus what they accomplished in the aftermath of the Revolution is all the more extraordinary, truly unexampled in the Atlantic world of their day. They could not write state constitutions or transform the political system under which white revolutionaries intended to live as an independent people. But the black founding fathers embarked on a project to accomplish what is almost always part of modern revolutionary agendas—to recast the social system.

In the northern states, African Americans and their white abolitionist allies tried to do this by capitalizing on the promise of the Revolution's most

radical pledge—to end slavery. Though a loosely orga-
nized national effort under the Articles of Confederation had accomplished independence, slavery had to
be combated state by state and even locale by locale
and person by person. Mostly, this antislavery crusade fell to the hands of free African Americans and
their white allies who lived in the North.

Leading them into the new era were a group of
mostly young men who became the rootstock of
postwar black society. Revolutions often call forth
talent at an unusually young age, but in this case the
talent had to emerge from a remnant of young African Americans because many of those in their teens
and twenties had fled to the British during the war.
Harry Hosier, born a slave in North Carolina in
about 1750, emerged by the early 1780s as an itinerating Methodist preacher with remarkable homi-
letic gifts—"the greatest orator in America," according to Philadelphia's sober-sided doctor Benjamin
Rush.[52] Peter Spence, born a slave in Maryland, was
twenty-three when he led black Methodists out of the
white church in Wilmington, Delaware, in 1805, and
Thomas Paul emerged as the most important
"exhorter" among black Bostonians in his early twenties. Daniel Coker, a Maryland slave, was only twenty-
five when he became the teacher of a Baltimore black

school, two years after he began preaching. He published a biting abolitionist pamphlet before his twenty-sixth birthday. Richard Allen began preaching to mostly white audiences and converting many of his hearers to Methodism at age twenty, only a few months after his release from slavery. In every seaport town—Boston, Providence, New Haven, New York, Philadelphia, Wilmington, Baltimore—young black founding fathers emerged. To this day they are still largely unnoticed in the schoolbooks from which young Americans learn their history.

Most of the young black leaders who ushered in the first era of freedom were not only largely self-taught but widely traveled. In an era of primitive transportation, and when their slender means usually precluded any form of travel other than on foot, many trekked thousands of miles and knew vast stretches of territory in ways that whites of their age seldom experienced. Richard Allen, later the founder of the African Methodist Episcopal Church, in his early twenties journeyed unceasingly for six years between South Carolina and New York and even into Indian country, making a living as woodcutter, shoemaker, and wagoner while preaching the gospel. The itinerating Methodist preachers Daniel Coker and Harry Hosier knew the entire region from New York to Baltimore. John Gloucester, a Tennessee slave who at age thirty-one became the leader of the first black Presbyterian church in Philadelphia, traveled for years up and down the Atlantic seaboard and across the Atlantic to England to collect money to free his family from slavery. Nero Prince, who became grand master of Boston's Black Masonic Lodge, traveled all over the world as a mariner and spent a dozen years as a footman at the court of the Russian czar in the early nineteenth century. Religious leaders such as David George, Lemuel Haynes, John Marrant, and John Chavis were likewise knowledgeable about regions as remote as Nova Scotia and the Cherokee towns of central and western Appalachia.

For most of these men, conversion to the Methodist or Baptist faith led them, after securing freedom, to a circuit-riding life. In something akin to biblical journeys into the wilderness, they tested their mettle and deepened their faith. In so doing they developed a toughness, a resiliency, an ability to confront rapidly changing circumstances, and a talent for dealing with a wide variety of people. This occurred more rarely among ordinary white citizens of the new republic, who were farm- and village-bound. Hence, in the post-revolutionary years, many of the most notable cases of self-made men ascending from society's

lowest rungs to positions of responsibility and influence involved recently freed slaves. These were the African Americans who reached manhood in the crucible of revolution and took up the work that the black leader William J. Wilson would call for half a century later: "We must begin to tell our own story, write our own lecture, paint our own picture, chisel our own bust . . . [and] acknowledge and love our own peculiarities."[53]

Two of them are illustrative and can stand for many others. Born in 1760, Richard Allen grew up as

*Gaol, in Walnut Street, Philadelphia.* William Birch engraving, 1799. The Library Company of Philadelphia.

Richard Allen purchased a blacksmith's shop in 1794, to be moved onto the city lot he purchased on Sixth Street in Philadelphia, where it would serve as the first "Mother Bethel Church." In 1799 William Birch portrayed a wooden building, mounted on a wheeled platform, being hauled away from the neighborhood of the Walnut Street Prison. Is it possible that Birch had heard about this event that was so important to black Philadelphians and wanted to add street action to his series of engravings of notable Philadelphia buildings? If so, why did he portray the workers hauling the building as white when probably most of them were black? Absent answers to these questions, historians continue to identify the blacksmith's shop as Richard Allen's first African Methodist Episcopal Church.

a slave to Benjamin Chew, a wealthy conservative lawyer in Philadelphia who maintained a plantation in
southern Delaware, where his labor force was mostly
enslaved. Chew sold Allen's family to a neighboring
Delaware farmer just before the Revolution, and it
was there that the slave known only as "Richard" experienced a religious conversion at the hands of itinerant Methodists. Contributing to the conversion,
one supposes, was the spiritual solace and a kind
of replacement family provided by the Methodists.
Richard's new master, Stokeley Sturgis, also felt the
power of the Methodist message. Nudged along by
economic strain in the war-torn economy, he let
Richard and his brother purchase their freedom.[54]

In 1780, with the war still raging, the twenty-year-
old Richard gave himself the surname of Allen and
began a six-year religious sojourn. Interspersing work
as woodcutter, a wagon driver carrying salt for the
revolutionary army, and a shoemaker with stints of
itinerant preaching, he trudged hundreds of miles to
preach before black and white audiences. In the mid-
1780s he attracted the attention of Francis Asbury,
who was about to become the first American Methodist bishop. Asbury sent Allen, only twenty-four
years old at the time, to Philadelphia to preach to the
free African Americans who worshiped at St. George

Methodist church—a rude, dirt-floored building in the German part of the city. Allen soon became the city's foremost black leader. In 1786, at age twenty-six, he was an instigator of the Free African Society, which ministered to the needs of people coming out of slavery; in 1792, the creator of one of the first independent black churches in the North; in 1794, the co-author of one of the first published black texts opposing slavery and white racism; in 1797, the organizer of Philadelphia's first black school; in 1816, the founder of a black denomination, the African Methodist Episcopal Church, that grew to the largest in the Christian world—what W. E. B. Du Bois would describe as "by long odds the vastest and most remarkable product of American Negro civilization."[55]

Allen's role as a shaper of thought, mover of minds, and builder of institutions was matched by few of his white contemporaries, and what he accomplished was done in the face of obstacles that most whites did not have to overcome. Never receiving formal education, not so much as one day in school, he became an accomplished and eloquent writer, penning and publishing sermons, tracts, addresses, and remonstrances; compiling a hymnal; and drafting articles of organization and governance for various organizations.

Farther north, in Massachusetts, Lemuel Haynes became an inspiration for aspiring African Americans. After the war he supported himself doing farm labor while preparing for a lifetime in the ministry. "One-time minute man," says John Saillant, his recent biographer, he "never wavered in his patriotism," and "he articulated more clearly than anyone of his generation, black or white, the abolitionist implications of republican thought." Haynes understood what half a million fellow African Americans were up against: that while early in the revolutionary struggle political leaders up and down the seaboard had agreed that slavery was an affront to the natural rights on which republicanism was built, as the war wound down the dominant theoreticians of republican ideology—men such as Thomas Jefferson and James Madison—began to view black people *themselves,* rather than the institution of slavery, as corrosive to "the great republican experiment." "The eradication of slavery," writes Saillant, "and the extension to blacks of the liberty and security of an antislavery republican state were, in Haynes's mind, essential to republican governance and republican life." A self-disciplined and modulated reformer, Haynes knew that many leaders revered for their roles in the struggle for independence were participants in the eva-

sion of the contradiction of black Americans perpetually trapped in slavery in the midst of the nascent
republic.[56]

Licensed to preach in 1780—this was the first ordi-
nation of a black clergyman by a largely white denomination in the United States—Haynes became
the spiritual leader of a white congregation in Middle Granville, Massachusetts. There he met Elizabeth
Babbitt, a white woman who bucked the tide of
prejudice against interracial marriage. Nine children
were born of this marriage, which lasted for more
than fifty years. One white minister, later to become
president of Amherst College, remembered that
Haynes sermonized with "no notes but spoke with
freedom and correctness . . . There was so much of
truth and nature in [his sermons] that hundreds
were melted into tears." In 1788 Haynes became the
pastor in Rutland, Vermont, where he served for
thirty years. It was there, in a state that had abolished
slavery in 1777, that his thoughts ripened on how
black Americans would fit into a republican scheme
of government. After Rutland, Haynes moved on to
his final pastorate in South Granville, New York,
where he served into the eighth decade of his life. After Haynes's death in 1833, his biographer called him
"a sanctified genius," a man whose life story could

"hardly fail to mitigate the unreasonable prejudices against the Africans in our land."[57]

If Lemuel Haynes's assumption of the pulpit in Rutland, Vermont, was a hopeful sign that the seed of a biracial democracy had been planted in the rocky hills of New England, a less optimistic scenario unfolded hundreds of miles to the south. For white revolutionaries, George Washington's unwavering leadership and determination to overcome all odds in the cause of freedom guaranteed him a place of honor in the annals of history. After the Constitution was written and ratified, it was fitting—almost obligatory—that he should return from private life at Mount Vernon to become the nation's first president, for most white Americans regarded Washington as the embodiment and essence of the Revolution. But for black Americans the failure of the revolutionary promise of an end to slavery came as a bitter disappointment. Though little of their inner thoughts can be recovered, shards of evidence tell us of their sorrow and resentment that Washington did not help make unalienable rights the rights of all. In the dramatic decisions of two of his most trusted and well-positioned slaves we can see how this resentment percolated to the surface, impelling them to strike out on their own to make real the essence of the African Americans' Revolution.

Hercules and Ona Judge were only two of the hundreds of slaves who labored on the Virginia plantations of Martha and George Washington; but they were two of only nine the Washingtons took with them to Philadelphia when that city became the nation's capital for a decade after 1790. Their decisions speak to the agency of the most dispossessed Americans of the new republic—those who refused, in the lengthening shadows of the revolutionary era, to wait for official action on the abolition of slavery. Though they represented only a tiny fraction of the enslaved, their resoluteness stood as a beacon for others to follow, and they were living reminders to all slaveowners of the precariousness of trying to hold human property in thrall.

Ona Judge, born to an enslaved seamstress at Mount Vernon and sired by a white indentured servant from Leeds, England, served Martha Washington from 1784, when the mixed-race girl was about ten years of age. Martha Washington took her to Philadelphia in 1790, when Ona was sixteen. Six years later Ona learned that Martha was planning to give her as a wedding present to Eliza Custis, the first lady's granddaughter. Ona fled the executive mansion—it stood where the new Liberty Bell Center opened in 2003—just before the Washingtons were to return to Mount Vernon for summer recess in 1796. Her days of helping the first lady dress and powder up for levees and state functions, running errands for her, and accompanying her on visits to the wives of political and diplomatic leaders were now at an end. Many years later she recalled to a journalist from *Granite Freedom,* a New Hampshire abolitionist paper: "I had friends among the colored people of Philadelphia, had my things carried there [to a waiting ship] before hand, and left while [the Washingtons] were at dinner."[58]

The Washingtons railed at the ingratitude of Ona Judge fleeing slavery—"without the least provocation," as Washington wrote. Ona's "thirst for compleat freedom," as she called it, did not register with the president. The Washingtons sent agents after her, to shackle her in Portsmouth, New Hampshire, where she had taken refuge, and bring her back or bargain her into returning. Hunted down, Ona sent word that, if guaranteed freedom, she would return out of affection for the Washington family. The first family refused. With several hundred of their enslaved Africans at stake, they feared that rewarding her flight from slavery with a grant of freedom would set "a dangerous precedent." At that, Ona Judge swore she "should rather suffer death than return to slavery." When Washington persisted, his agent in Portsmouth reported in September 1796 that "popular opinion here is in favor of universal freedom," which made it difficult for him to seize and shackle Ona without a public outcry. Two years later the Washington family was still trying to snag Martha's ingrate chambermaid by surreptitiously sending George's nephew, Burwell Bassett, after her. Not until Washington's death in 1799 could Ona feel some measure of safety. By then she had married, had a baby, and put down roots in New Hampshire, where she lived out her life, poor but free.[59]

Nine months after Ona Judge's escape, just as the Washingtons were leaving Philadelphia to take up life as private citizens on their beloved Mt. Vernon plantation, another part of their human property declared his independence. To the Washingtons, Hercules enjoyed a special status in the executive mansion, one that in their view should have immunized him against the fever for freedom. As their prize cook, he had prepared countless state dinners over a number of years, a man "as highly accomplished and proficient in the culinary art as could be found in the

United States."[60] But Hercules, like Ona Judge, had mingled with numerous free black Philadelphians, who by this time had built two churches of their own, started schools and mutual aid societies, carved out niches in the urban economy, even purchased homes, and begun mounting attacks on the fortress of slavery. The promise of the American Revolution stood before his eyes.

Hercules doffed his chef's bonnet, slipped away from the president's house, melted into the countryside, made his way to New York, and outwitted all of Washington's attempts to capture him. When Louis-Philippe, later the king of France, visited Mount Vernon shortly after this, he asked Hercules' six-year-old daughter whether she was brokenhearted at the prospect of never seeing her father again. "Oh sir!" she replied, "I am very glad because he is free now."[61]

Washington had feared such escapes since his arrival in Philadelphia. He had written to his secretary Tobias Lear in 1791 that he did not think his slaves "would be benefited" by achieving freedom, "yet the idea of freedom might be too great a temptation to resist." Breathing the free air of Philadelphia, where the pesky Quakers were helping enslaved Pennsylvanians break their shackles, might "make them insolent in a state of slavery." Near the end of his presi-

*Presumed Cook of George Washington.* Copyright © Museo Thyssen-Bornemisza, Madrid.

Art historians are still struggling to identify the artist who painted this striking image of Hercules, Washington's head chef, but it is attributed tentatively to Gilbert Stuart. In 1797, at the end of his master's presidency, Hercules made his own declaration of independence by fleeing the Washingtons' executive mansion in Philadelphia. Washington never tracked down his escaped slave, and historians have found no traces of Hercules' later life. A superb culinary artist, Hercules ran the first family's kitchen with such a commanding presence that "his underlings flew in all directions" when he issued orders.

dency, and still grating at Ona Judge's flight, he ordered his secretary to get his slaves back to Mount Vernon. Mindful that the pursuit of freedom-loving slaves would tarnish his reputation on both sides of the Atlantic, he instructed Lear: "I wish to have it accomplished under a pretext that may deceive both them and the public. I request that these sentiments and this advice may be known to none but yourself and Mrs. Washington."[62]

Washington's desire to avoid the appearance of a severe slaveowner bent on hunting down escaped slaves, brought to a head by the flight of Ona Judge and Hercules, may have figured in his decision to free his one hundred twenty-four slaves in his will (the dower slaves Martha had brought to the marriage were her sole property and therefore beyond the reach of her husband's wishes). If two of the most advantaged household slaves would take flight, was there any such thing as a reliable slave? Martha Washington certainly knew this too. She freed her husband's slaves one year after his death in 1799 rather than making them wait and hope for her own death; she knew that to hold them any longer was to invite an untimely death at the hands of a black man or woman who would thereby instantly become the liberator of one hundred twenty-four slaves.[63]

For African Americans, a revolution within a revolution had occurred, and they rightfully considered *their* "glorious cause" to be the purest form of the "spirit of '76." White American revolutionaries were animated by a thirst for independence and freedom, by a determination to overthrow corrupt power, by a willingness to die for unalienable rights, by a resolve to defend the people's power against all odds as the ultimate source of authority. All this was ennobling and inspiring and has stood forth to this day around the world as the meaning of their blood sacrifice. Black American revolutionaries could salute every one of these white banners but with a difference: a thirst for freedom which involved unshackled bodies as well as political ideals; a determination to end corrupt power as they experienced it at the end of a whip and at the stake; a willingness to die for unalienable rights against odds even greater than those faced by white revolutionaries. From this perspective, the African Americans' Revolution had only begun as the white patriots' Revolution ended in victory after eight years of war.

## 2

## COULD SLAVERY
## HAVE BEEN ABOLISHED?

FOR GENERATIONS, white historians have taken for
granted that it would not have been possible to abolish slavery during the revolutionary era. In 1976, as
the nation was celebrating the bicentennial of the
American Revolution, it was commonplace to com-
mend the founding fathers for *not* attempting to end
slavery, a step regarded as hopelessly idealistic if not
fanatical. Why fanatical? Partly, it is argued, because
"only gradually were [white] men coming to see that
[slavery] was a peculiarly degrading and a uniquely
brutalizing institution"—a "dawning awareness" that
only crept up on the revolutionary generation.[1] Research in recent years about the roots and extent of
abolitionist thought, led by David Brion Davis, has
demolished this notion that it was beyond the cognitive reach of the founders to imagine that they could
eliminate slavery. We now understand that abolitionist sentiment was widespread, though of course un-

evenly, throughout the new nation. David Waldstreicher, in a recent survey of the literature, con-
cludes that "a consensus existed in many, perhaps
most parts of the country, that slavery was inconsistent with American revolutionary principles and
ought to be consigned to the dustbin of history."[2]

But the main reason offered for calling antislavery
efforts "fanatical" is the argument that any attempt
to prohibit slavery would have shattered the newly
formed union of states that had won independence
from Great Britain. The intransigence of Georgia and
South Carolina would have guaranteed that—or so
the argument goes. In such a situation, idealism had
to be tempered with pragmatism, with pragmatism
trumping idealism in any showdown. Thus, even if
ending slavery had emerged as a key element of a revolutionary reform agenda, a campaign on its behalf
could not have surmounted the threat of disunion.

The argument that slavery could *not* have been
abolished reeks of the dangerous, indeed odious,
concept of historical inevitability, almost always in
historical writing a concept advanced by those eager
to excuse mistakes and virtually never by those writing on behalf of victims of the mistakes. The idea of
historical inevitability is a winner's weapon, as old as
the tales told by ancient conquerors. The philoso-

pher Isaiah Berlin puts it cogently: "The behaviour of men is . . . made what it is by factors largely beyond the control of individuals . . . Our sense of guilt and of sin, our pangs of remorse and self-condemnation, are automatically dissolved; the tension, the fear of failure and frustration disappear as we become aware of the elements of a larger 'organic whole,' of which we are variously described as limbs or elements . . . Viewed in this new light [our historical actions] turn out no longer wicked but right and good because necessitated."[3]

It is time to reconsider the entire matter. The proper starting point is a brief review of five interlocking factors in the 1780s and early 1790s that made the immediate post-revolutionary period an opportune time for abolishing slavery. First, it was the era when the sentiment for ridding American society of a blood-drenched labor system widely agreed to be an insult to the Revolution's sponsorship of universal rights was at its peak. Beginning with Pennsylvania, Vermont, and Massachusetts, northern state legislatures and supreme courts were outlawing slavery— gradually, to be sure, but with moral certitude. As for Maryland and Virginia, the region with the greatest number of slaves, Jefferson believed that "from the mouth to the head of the Chesapeake, the bulk of the people will approve of [extirpating slavery] in theory, and it will find a respectable minority ready to adopt it in practice, a minority which for weight and worth of character preponderates against the great number, who have not the courage to divest their families of a property which however keeps their consciences unquiet."[4] North Carolina, in 1790, insisted that slavery be banned from the western lands it was ceding to the national government. In both North and South, religious leaders, particularly those of the fast-growing Baptists and Methodists, were speaking forthrightly about the necessity of cleansing the country of a national sin. Larry Tise, in a survey of proslavery thought, found that from 1775 to the early nineteenth century almost no southern leader defended slavery.[5]

Second, this was the moment when the part of the new nation most resistant to abolition, the Lower South, was also composed of the two states most precariously situated and ill-prepared to break away from the rest of the nation, a topic to be pursued below. Third, it was a period when the system of thought called cultural environmentalism was in full sway. Nobody contested the deplorable state of enslaved Africans, but their pitiable condition, according to environmentalist thought, was caused not by nature—biological inferiority—but by lack of nurture, a systematic denial of uplifting education or opportunities to improve themselves, along with brutal treatment that extinguished sparks of genius. No inborn disability, argued the environmentalists, stood in the way of emancipation, which, when accomplished, would allow the flowering of black talent and responsible behavior.

Fourth, the opening of the trans-Appalachian West after England surrendered its claims to this vast territory provided the wherewithal for a compensated emancipation. This would have been expensive, but even as early as 1775 a Connecticut clergyman had shown in great detail how that state could use its western lands to indemnify all its slaveowners at a relatively modest cost.[6] Vastly more slaves lived in the South, but even if no southern state would commit public resources to effect a compensated emancipation, the sale of western lands, ceded by the states to the federal government, "promised virtually inexhaustible revenues," as our leading historian of western lands tells us, "to promote the common interests of all the states and strengthen the national government." With independence assured in 1783, many political leaders, including Jefferson, promoted the use of hundreds of million acres of "the richest wild lands in the world" to underwrite the creation of "an empire of liberty." Sold at two dollars per acre, the land would have yielded enough to purchase the freedom of every adult slave in the country, ensuring that a true empire of liberty would supplant an empire of slavery.[7] Using the western domain as an instrument for binding the nation together was much in the public mind in the 1780s. Many concerned leaders also contemplated using this immense area as a sanctuary where freed men and women could be resettled if public opinion would not permit them to remain in the already settled parts of the country. This would have mimicked the way the British had relocated former American slaves in Nova Scotia at the end of the war and begun transporting free blacks in London and other English cities to Sierra Leone by 1786.

Lastly, the outbreak of black rebellion in Saint Domingue in 1791 and the thunderclap decision of the French Revolutionary government in February 1794 to emancipate half a million slaves, along with the almost simultaneous passage of a bill in England's House of Commons to abolish the English slave trade, led to a crescendo of antislavery radicalism by the mid-1790s. As Washington started his second term as president, the belief spread that the entire western world was poised to reverse the sordid three-century descent into European-sponsored enslavement of Africans. In the view of many, the time seemed at hand, as the poet-journalist Philip Freneau expressed it, when "philosophy and religion shall deliver a suffering race from those evils; and when the gradual progress of reason will unite nation with nation, and colour with colour, blending the rights of man with the expectations of policy and commerce."[8]

Let us now turn to the argument central to the defense of the revolutionary generation's failure to abolish slavery—that the nation's frailty would not permit such a fundamental change. No one doubts that the confederation of thirteen American states was imperfectly knit together; indeed, for this reason the Americans barely won the war of independence, and only, as it happened, with massive French and Dutch aid. But how could the union of states be strengthened? Pondering the tenuousness of the post-revolutionary confederation of states, historians have seldom considered that a national plan for abolishing slavery might have been an *integrative* rather than a *divisive* mechanism. Is it a counterfactual flight of fantasy that ending slavery might have helped create a genuinely national society out of semi-separate, fractious regions? Is it not possible that this could have bolstered union by eliminating a rankling sore in the body politic and completing a reform without which postwar American society could never be ideologically true to itself? Is it not true that any society where people's behavior aligns with their principles is stronger than one in which practice and principles are at odds?

English writers, even before the war, were arguing that the gradual abolition of slavery would make the empire more secure and promote civic harmony, which would forever elude societies filled with slaves.[9] Americans, of course, were privy to these publications as part of a transatlantic community of letters. The application of such thinking to the budding American "empire of liberty" was natural enough, and it appears in the foreboding of many Americans after the war that the new nation could not survive if it abandoned principles widely subscribed to during its blood-filled birth. It is likely that a national referendum would have supported the proposition of Maryland's Luther Martin in 1788 that "slavery is inconsistent with the genius of republicanism, and has a tendency to destroy those principles on which it is supported, as it lessens the sense of the equal rights of mankind and habituates us to tyranny and oppression." Martin was not an ascetic Quaker, an eccentric visionary, or a northerner, but a highly respected delegate to the Constitutional Convention. He directed these remarks, which pinpointed slavery as a main contributor to political fragility, amidst heated debates in Maryland over ratifying the Constitution. "It ought to be considered," he advised, "that national crimes can only be, and frequently are, punished in this world by national punishments, and that the continuance of the slave trade, and thus giving it a national sanction and encouragement ought to be considered as justly exposing us to the displeasure and vengeance of Him, who is equal Lord of all, and who views with equal eye, the poor African slave and his American master." Martin withdrew from the Constitutional Convention and refused to sign the document because he regarded the three-fifths compromise—by which three-fifths of slaves were to be counted in a state's population to determine representation in Congress—and the protection of the slave trade as "a solemn mockery of, and insult to that God whose protection we had . . . implored, and could not fail to hold us up in detestation, and render us contemptible to every true friend of liberty in the world."[10]

Was Luther Martin an isolated southerner in believing that without the abolition of slavery the nation would never coalesce but would be left impaired and divided? Far from it. The documentary record is dotted with expressions of the conviction that trying to maintain a republic of slaveholders would nearly guarantee a cataclysm. It was a staple of political thinking that aristocracy and slavery were braided together, just as freedom and democracy were intertwined. In 1798, when he was planning a will that would free scores of slaves after his death, Washington told an English visitor that only "the rooting out of slavery can perpetuate the existence of our union, by consolidating it in a common bond of principle."[11] Three years later, shortly after stepping down as Virginia's last Federalist governor, James Wood agreed to serve as president of the Virginia Abolition Society, and he served on the state's Council of State until his death in 1816, showing that the spirit of abolitionism was far from dead in Virginia.

The thought that the continued existence of slavery could wreck the republican dream and divide the republic also tormented James Madison, the chief architect of the Constitution. Like Washington, Madison knew all about what he called the "grievous wrongs" inflicted on slaves. But morality and humanitarianism were less important to Madison than the way slavery tore at the fabric and unity of the new nation. By keeping one-fifth of its people enslaved, the American republic weakened itself militarily, presenting "a standing invitation to foreign intrigue" and making the nation perpetually vulnerable to invasion (as the War of 1812 would prove). Even in economic terms, Madison believed, slavery represented a national weakness rather than a national strength because slaves were less productive than free laborers. Nor could the new United States expect to exert moral force abroad while slavery stained the republic. And most of all, for Madison, "slavery raised the ominous specter of a regional polarization . . . that might jeopardize [the revolutionary] generation's greatest achievement." In other words, ending slavery would *unify*, not irreparably split, the nation because the death of slavery would prevent sectionalism from reaching such a pitch that union was no longer possible.[12]

The second objection to the argument that political fragility made it impossible to abolish slavery concerns the belligerent opposition of South Carolina and Georgia to all attempts at abolition. Historians who believe that slavery could not have been eliminated in the revolutionary era are specially fond of quoting the ultimatum thrown down by South Carolina's delegate to the Continental Congress,

Thomas Lynch, and the state's delegate to the Constitutional Convention, John Rutledge. "If slavery was debated," stormed Lynch just after the signing of the Declaration of Independence, "whether their slaves are their property, there is an end of the Confederation." Thirteen years later, at the Constitutional Convention, Rutledge declared that the "true question at present is whether the Southern States shall or shall not be parties to the Union."[13] We need not fault historians for reporting this militant defense of slavery in the Lower South, for the defense was real. But historians have not adequately considered whether these two states were truly in a position to dictate national policy on this crucial issue. This proposition bows to the notion that the weak can control the powerful.

In fact, Georgia and South Carolina were precariously situated in 1787 and needed a strong federal government far more than the rest of the states needed them. The fabric of Georgia's backcountry had been grievously torn by the time the war ended, four years before the Constitutional Convention.[14] General William Moultrie, riding one hundred miles eastward from the backcountry in 1782, described a countryside previously flush with "live-stock and wild fowl of every kind, . . . Now destitute of all . . .

not the vestiges of horses, cattle, hogs, or deer was to be found. The squirrels and birds of every kind were totally destroyed." It is no surprise, given this devastation, that rice and indigo production from 1783 to 1786 stood at half the level in 1770–1773. Likewise, South Carolina on the eve of the Constitutional Convention was struggling with a wrenching debt crisis while staggered by the loss of tens of thousands of slaves through death and flight to the British during the war years. The Palmetto state, like Georgia, was so "ravaged by war," as the military historian Don Higginbotham tells us, that "its governmental processes had collapsed and its society had disintegrated to the point that it approached John Locke's savage state of nature."[15]

After the war, when the British closed their West Indies colonies to American ships, both southern states were further hamstrung and isolated, all the more in the need of inclusion in a nationwide economic compact. And then, while they nursed their strangled economies back to health, their Creek Indian neighbors threatened their very existence. In 1786 the emergence of the mixed-race leader Alexander McGillivray as a Great Beloved Man unified the fractious Creeks. Leading war parties against Georgia frontiersmen who had poured into the Creeks' ancient homelands, McGillivray threw the state "entirely on the defensive." Armed by the Spanish, the Creeks "swept the [back]country clean" in 1786 and drove out returning frontiersmen the next summer. As the Constitutional Convention got under way, South Carolinians and Georgians trembled at the prospect of a pan-Indian alliance in the backcountry because McGillivray had just entertained a delegation of headmen from western tribes in the Ohio country. Georgia even convened a special session of the legislature to deal with the emergency. No wonder that George Washington remarked: "If a weak state, with powerful tribes of Indians in its rear and the Spaniards on its flank, do not incline to embrace a strong general government, there must, I should think, be either wickedness or insanity in their conduct."[16]

No doubt wickedness existed aplenty in Georgia, but insanity there was not. Georgia's ratification convention rushed pell-mell to endorse the Constitution unanimously, almost without debate. They did so, said the state's representative to Congress in 1789, "in full confidence that a good, complete, and efficient government would succor and relieve them [from the Creeks and Spanish]."[17] This desperate condition of Georgia and South Carolina makes their threats to withdraw from the new nation if the Constitution addressed the issue of slavery ring hollow.

Granting the intense commitment to slavery among Georgians and Carolinians, what might have happened if the other states had not accommodated them on the issue? To be sure, on the eve of the Constitutional Convention many politicians talked of separate confederacies (northern, mid-Atlantic, and southern); but most of this was rhetorical posturing, a game of blind man's bluff. None of the stratagems for breaking up the nation received serious consideration. Among all the bluffers, South Carolina and Georgia, still reeling from internecine revolutionary war and Indian enemies, were in the worst position to strike out on their own. Would they have established a Deep South nation of their own? As part of Catholic Spain's American empire? Or as part of a British West Indies confederacy, embracing the country against which they had fought? None of these was remotely possible. The war had shown the Lower South's military weakness and its dependence on the states to its north for protection. Edward Rutledge admitted in 1788 that South Carolina, "in the day of danger," must rely "on the naval force of our northern friends."[18]

And if South Carolina and Georgia had recklessly

seceded from the union, would the rest of the states have been deeply damaged? Hardly. They would have lost a paltry five or six percent of the nation's population. The two southernmost states had caused general disgust during the Revolution by contributing nothing at all to the fiscal quotas set by Congress. When the British moved the war south in 1779, governors in those states were dismally unsuccessful in turning out militiamen, even when Savannah and Charleston fell to the British. The rumor in 1780 that Georgia and South Carolina, invaded by the British and caught up in a maelstrom of civil war, would surrender to Great Britain to gain peace brought no cries of distress from the northern delegates to Congress.

By the late 1780s most southerners admitted privately that even the entire South could not make it on its own. A comment by James Monroe of Virginia a year before the Constitutional Convention convened, at a time when the issue of free navigation on the Mississippi created a North-South crisis, is revealing. If the confederation fell apart over this issue, Monroe opined, it would be essential that Pennsylvania join the South.[19] Tench Coxe, a leading political economist of the period, made the same point in 1790 by showing how thoroughly the Upper South was commercially dependent on links to the northern states.

As it turned out, Georgians and South Carolinians did not have to decide how to respond if the other states took a forceful position on the slave trade and slavery. To their delight, northerners and Chesapeake leaders who had argued that a republic could not be built upon a foundation of coerced labor proved willing to live with the contradiction between slavery and republicanism. The source of this willingness was not the aces held in the hand of Georgia and South Carolina but the unwillingness of the northern states to participate in solving the problem of slavery.

If historians have been reluctant to question whether Georgia and South Carolina were really in a position to convince the other states that their secession would cripple the new nation, they have also been reluctant to consider how much responsibility the northern and upper southern states bore for the exhaustion of the abolitionist movement by the end of the eighteenth century. Some have justified this studied inattention by pointing out that northern states banned further importation of slaves (as did most southern states) and passed gradual abolition laws. This much they could do, according to this argument, but nothing more, leaving the South as the home of the system of compelled labor. For many decades, historians educated and teaching mostly at northern universities have gotten the North off the hook by arguing that slavery in the post-revolutionary era was a southern problem rather than a national one.

This line of argument is a bit self-congratulatory and more than a bit narrow of vision. The northern gradual abolition laws were indeed important, signifying legislators' admission that slavery was fundamentally incompatible with the principles upon which they erected their new state governments. Yet most northern slaves slipped their shackles only by dying or running away, while their children got freedom only after long periods of indentured servitude, usually twenty-eight years. Perhaps more important, northern antislavery sentiment translated poorly into willingness to bear responsibility for concrete steps for abolishing it. Jefferson may have been right that opponents of antislavery in the North were no more numerous than the occasional murderers and robbers who roamed the countryside, but his prediction in 1785 that "in a few years there will be no slaves northward of Maryland" was too optimistic. And most northerners refused to recognize slavery as a problem that Americans in every region of the country, not just southerners, must address. Many of those who spoke about national destiny—about creating an "empire of liberty," in Jefferson's memorable phrase—did recognize that as a national problem, slavery required a national solution in which the northern states might have been expected to participate fully. As Madison would say some years later, in authoring his own emancipation scheme, "it is the nation which is to reap the benefit [of emancipation]. The nation, therefore, ought to bear the burden."[20]

It became all too evident at the Constitutional Convention that the Revolution's leaders, while providing a new frame of national government that capped their revolutionary war achievements, were backing away from what many knew was essential to create "a more perfect union." This pregnant phrase that opened the Constitution was followed by five clauses protecting slavery, and this ensured that the delegates created a *less* perfect union. Northern pocketbook tenderness trumped conscience when the New England representatives traded their support for protecting the slave trade for twenty years for southern support for eliminating all but incidental state duties on exports, a boon to the shipping-oriented northern states.[21] Most northern as well as southern delegates acted with the hope that they were burying the issue of ending slavery. Yet even the most talented political theorists could not make the resentment and disappointment of half a million enslaved people disappear.

Sidestepping the slavery issue at the Constitutional Convention by no means removed the harsh realities of slavery from public discourse. In 1790 the first Congress to sit under the ratified constitution found itself beset with Quaker and Pennsylvania Abolition Society petitions, filled with forthright language about "the gross national iniquity of trafficking in the persons of fellow-men." Debate on this delayed Congress's work on Hamilton's Report on Public Credit—the plan to assume and fund the revolutionary war debts of the states. Though hardly mentioned in textbook accounts of the first Congress, these petitions produced a full-scale debate on slavery and the power of the nation's government to ameliorate it. The House of Representatives appointed a special committee by a vote of forty-three to eleven, with Maryland and Virginia representatives backing a full consideration of the petitions. The resulting press coverage brought the issue squarely before the public. Though the "general spirit of the [committee's] report was antislavery," according to its principal student, it led to no congressional action and was vitiated by Madison's key assertion that Congress had "no authority to interfere in the emancipation of slaves, or in the treatment of them."[22]

Yet the issue of abolishing slavery remained very much alive. One indication was the commencement debate at the College of New Jersey in 1792. The intellectual jousting between the two graduating seniors was not about whether abolition was the right course for the nation to follow—this was a given—but about whether slaves should be emancipated without being prepared for freedom "by a proper education to be good citizens." A weightier occasion followed when the newly recognized state of Kentucky elected delegates to write a constitution. Among the elected delegates were six passionately antislavery clergymen, led by the Presbyterian leader David Rice, and ten others determined to cleanse Kentucky of slavery. Set against them were twenty-six proslavery delegates, most of them Virginians who had moved into the bluegrass region. Roger Kennedy reasons that "a little weight on the antislavery side . . . might have swung things the other way," for the western frontier, filled with evangelical Presbyterians, Methodists, and

Baptists, "was ripe for the politics of conscience and hungry for leadership."[23]

Moreover, schemes for emancipating the growing number of slaves kept popping up in the early 1790s, occasioning vigorous debate. Ferdinando Fairfax, Washington's Virginia neighbor and protégé, floated one in 1790, and an unnamed author proposed an emancipation scheme in Baltimore in the same year. Another came from Virginia's constitutional scholar St. George Tucker in 1796. All of these plans recognized the ocean of white prejudice against black people and knew that any emancipation would have to be phased rather than immediate and total; but all assumed that slavery must be abolished if the nation was to stand firm under its new constitution. More debatable than abolishing slavery was what to do with emancipated slaves—an issue contested at this very time in England, where abolitionists were repatriating freedmen and women scattered around the English empire to the colony of Sierra Leone on Africa's western coast.[24]

In sum, the problem was neither a lack of energy among advocates of abolitionism nor a lack of concrete plans for the gradual obliteration of slavery nor a general unwillingness to condemn slavery. The missing element was strong leadership on a crucial issue. One of the lessons of history is that, in cases where a fundamental change has been accomplished against heavy odds, inspired leadership has been critically important. In such cases, those in pivotal positions of power have been willing to embrace controversy, incur the wrath of opponents, and sacrifice amiability, politeness, and even friendship in order to achieve a goal dictated by conscience. They have persuaded a resistant public rather than succumbing to it, even facing political ruin with honor.[25] "We want Founding Fathers," writes Joyce Appleby, "who summon us to a civic calling greater than going to the polls and paying taxes." One term for this is political courage. Virtually every book on the American Revolution stresses military, political, and diplomatic leadership as a key factor in the successful quest for independence and in the creation of structures of democratic government. Yet our history books are strangely silent on the failure of leadership regarding an abolitionist agenda that was overwhelmingly supported by many of Jefferson and Washington's closest European and American friends—the cosmopolitan, transatlantic so-called republic of letters. When political courage was most needed to solve the infant republic's greatest problem, the nation's leaders in the North and the Upper South failed to lead. This failure allowed the blunting of revolutionary reform that reached its climax in the mid-1790s and thereafter entered a period of eclipse.[26]

In the North, Benjamin Franklin and John Adams were two figures who had chances to make a crucial difference. Many of their friends loathed slavery and saw it as a malignant cancer eating at the nation's moral and political innards. Others, such as Pennsylvania's James Wilson, one of the architects of the Constitution, believed that "the abolition of slavery is within the reach of the federal government" and expected that Congress will "exterminate slavery from within our borders."[27] Franklin and Adams both admired the many clergymen and reformers pushing the abolitionist agenda. But beyond admiration beckoned alliance and activism. Crippling gout and kidney stones stripped Franklin of his unforgettable energy and insouciance, and to his credit he agreed to become president of the Pennsylvania Abolition Society in 1787 after it reorganized to launch a more muscular antislavery campaign directed at the Congress soon to meet if the states ratified the new Constitution. Franklin also lent his name to the petition to the first Congress in 1790 to immediately abolish the slave trade. And three weeks before his death in April 1790, he published a slashing, satiric attack on slavery, in which he likened southern slaveowners to Algerian pirates who sold captured white Christian sailors into bondage. But Franklin published this essay anonymously.[28] Of all the founding fathers, he exerted himself the most on behalf of abolition, yet he used only part of the vast reserve of credit he had amassed with the public.

The case of John Adams is different. His political influence and fund of respect from much of the public might not have moved political leaders in the South, where most slaves lived, but he could certainly have helped convince the North that its contributions toward a compensated emancipation were essential to solving what was not just a sectional but a truly national problem. While Franklin was failing by the late 1780s, Adams's star was rising. Some Adams biographers, most recently David McCullough, contend that Adams was "utterly opposed to slavery and the slave trade and . . . favored a gradual emancipation of all slaves." In fact, it was Abigail Adams who was "utterly opposed to slavery"; it was Abigail who expressed herself freely to this effect; and it was John who did his best to keep antislavery *off* the patriot reform agenda, sidetracking a gradual abolition bill in the Massachusetts legislature in 1777 and studiously ignoring the opportunity to follow Pennsyl-

vania's gradual abolition act of 1780 when he served
as main author of the Massachusetts constitution of
1780.[29]

After the Revolution, Adams did nothing to hurry
slavery to extinction. Abigail urged him to oppose
slavery more forcefully, but her husband never publicly risked any of his capital, either as vice president
or as president. In 1795, while vice president, he admitted with startling frankness that slavery was "a
subject to which I have never given any particular attention." Seven months later, Adams thought about
an emancipation plan being drafted by St. George
Tucker of Virginia and reached the conclusion that
"justice to the negroes would require that they
should not be abandoned by their masters and
turned loose upon a world in which they have no ca-
pacity to procure even a subsistence."[30] In taking this
position that mirrored those of the most hard-core
opponents of abolition, Adams turned his mind away
from the free black communities in Boston, New
York, and Philadelphia, of which he had personal
knowledge, that were establishing schools, churches,
mutual aid associations, and supporting themselves.
As president, Adams did reopen trade in 1799 with
the black Haitian revolutionists led by Toussaint-
Louverture, a measure mainly meant to gratify north-

ern merchants; but Adams kept his silence on the several emancipation schemes floated in the 1790s.[31]

Southern leaders, especially Virginia's Washington, Jefferson, and Madison, were strategically positioned to take the lead on the slavery issue. All three professed a hatred of slavery and a fervent desire to see it ended in their own time. As president, as secretary of state and then vice president, and as floor leader in the House of Representatives, Washington, Jefferson, and Madison knew of their unusual leverage as opinion shapers and political persuaders. And they recognized that some of their closest colleagues, including George Mason, Patrick Henry, George Wythe, Arthur Lee, Robert Carter, Ferdinando Fairfax, and Edmund Pendleton, publicly supported the gradual abolition of slavery. The three key Virginians were what Rogers Smith calls "ex-colonial nation builders" eager "to show their British former governors, and indeed all the haughty Europeans, that Americans could create a previously undreamed of enlightened republic." In this milieu, "active support of gradual emancipation by Washington, Jefferson, and Madison," writes John Kaminski, "might have been sufficient to mount a serious attack on slavery."[32]

What also might have encouraged them to gird

their loins and become resolute leaders was the readiness of Virginia's two leading lawyer-judges, George Wythe and St. George Tucker, to mend the nation's torn Achilles' heel. Both were friends and confidants of Washington, Jefferson, and Madison. Descended from George Keith, Pennsylvania governor and one of the earliest antislavery advocates in North America, Wythe married into one of Virginia's elite slaveowning families, signed the Declaration of Independence, and had a reputation second to none in Virginia as a paragon of virtue and learning. He had been Jefferson's law mentor and remained "his most affectionate friend throughout life." Wythe had come to hate slavery by the time he received appointment as professor of law and police at William and Mary College in 1779. His "sentiments on the subject of slavery are unequivocal," Jefferson wrote to the English abolitionist leader Richard Price in 1785, and he preached the doctrine of antislavery to "all the young men of Virginia under preparation for public life."[33] After his wife's death in 1787, Wythe began divesting himself of the slaves she had brought to their marriage and freed four of them. Stepping down in 1790 from the William and Mary faculty, Wythe moved to Virginia's highest court, where he ruled in 1801 in favor of freedom for an enslaved woman and her children, and made "some sweeping assertions about the inconsistency of slavery with the first article of Virginia's Declaration of Rights."[34]

St. George Tucker, who succeeded Wythe as William and Mary's law professor in 1790, was equally certain that the United States could never fulfill its destiny of leading the world's nations toward freedom while clasping the viper of slavery to its bosom. Married into the slave- and land-rich Bland-Randolph families, Tucker had led Virginia militia troops and fought alongside the Marquis de Lafayette when British commanders Benedict Arnold and Banastre Tarleton plundered Virginia in 1781. Tucker had seen some of his wife's slaves and many of his in-laws' slaves escape to the British during that harrowing year. After the war, he knew that many of Virginia's most distinguished families were wallowing in debt as their slaves worked unprofitably on land-exhausted tobacco plantations. A mutiny at one of his in-laws' plantations in 1787 heightened his disgust with slavery.[35] By 1790 Tucker was having William and Mary students examine the "inconsistency between our avowed principles and practices" and "whether it is practicable to wipe off that stigma [of slavery] from our nation and government." Four years later he was sharing a gradual abolition plan with his students; he published this scheme two years after that. Tucker's advocacy of gradual abolition did not prevent his appointment to the Virginia Court of Appeals in 1804 or to the U.S. District Court in Virginia in 1813.[36] In sum, the two powerhouse legal minds of Virginia in the 1780s and 1790s, operating at the state's intellectual nerve center at William and Mary and on the bench of the state's highest court, were staunchly determined to eradicate slavery. Washington, Jefferson, and Madison knew that they could count on the support of these two men if they deigned to step forward on the slavery issue.

Washington, as Henry Wiencek has shown, had been troubled ever since seeing black soldiers fighting valiantly for the American cause. He called slavery "the foul stain of manhood" and contemplated, as the war drew to an end, whether he might be the key figure in securing the unalienable rights of man. Pushing him hard was the dashing young Marquis de Lafayette, who had become far more to Washington than a comrade-in-arms amidst the din of war, virtually an adopted son for the childless general.[37]

After the war the French nobleman acted on earlier talks with Washington about rooting slavery out of America. When word reached Lafayette in Spain that American and British negotiators had signed a preliminary peace treaty in January 1783, he dispatched a French ship to carry the news to Congress. Including a letter of congratulations to "our beloved matchless Washington," Lafayette proposed that the nation's conquering hero join him in an experiment to free all their slaves. Lafayette would purchase an estate in French Guiana, and there they would settle their slaves and prepare them for freedom. "Such an example as yours might render it a general practice," wrote Lafayette, and he even imagined that "if we succeed in America," he would devote himself to spreading the experiment to the West Indies. "If it be a wild scheme," Lafayette concluded, "I had rather be mad this way than to be thought wise in the other tack."[38]

Washington did not dismiss the idea, knowing he might be the exemplar for others to follow. "I shall be happy to join you in so laudable a work," he told Lafayette, and added that he would welcome seeing his surrogate son to discuss the details "of the business." Lafayette indeed visited Mount Vernon in 1784, and they discussed the experiment. William Gordon, an antislavery Boston minister who was at the time writing one of the first histories of the American Revolution, recalled after visiting Mount Vernon that Washington "wished to get rid of his Negroes, and the Marquis wished that an end might be put to the slavery of all of them." In a letter to Washington, Gordon urged that he use his enormous clout, so that, teamed with Lafayette, "your joint counsels and influence" might accomplish emancipation, "and thereby give the finishing stroke and the last polish to your political characters."[39]

Nine months later, in May 1785, the Methodist leaders Francis Asbury and Thomas Coke visited Mount Vernon to solicit Washington's support for a petition they would deliver to Virginia's House of Delegates urging a gradual emancipation of slaves. They knew that Washington's fortitude and integrity had taken root in America's heart and nowhere more so than in Virginia. Washington reiterated his wish to end slavery and told the Methodists that he "had signified his thoughts on the subject to most of the great men of the state." He declined to sign the petition but promised to "signify his sentiments to the Assembly by letter" if they "took it into consideration." Virginia's legislature did take the petition under consideration in November 1785, shortly after one planter—Joseph Mayo—had freed more than one hundred fifty slaves. The legislature rejected the petition, though not, according to James Madison, "without an avowed patronage of its principle by sundry respectable members." Among the supporters was George Wythe, Jefferson's yoke-mate in overhauling Virginia's code of laws during the Revolution. Contrary to his promise, Washington did not write the letter supporting a gradual abolition of slavery.[40]

Later that year, Robert Pleasants of Virginia again appealed to Washington's "fame in being the successful champion of American liberty." Pleasants was from an old-stock Virginia family of slaveowning Quakers, and by the time of the Revolution he was convinced that he should free his slaves. This became possible only after Virginia made such manumissions legal in 1782—a measure that led many Virginians, including some of Washington's neighbors, to free some ten thousand slaves in the 1780s and twenty thousand before the end of the century. Pleasants also worked to obtain the freedom of the many slaves that his deceased father and brother had emancipated in their wills five years before but had placed in the service of their heirs.[41] "It seems highly probable to me," he wrote to Washington, "that thy example and influence at this time towards a general emancipation would be as productive of real happiness to mankind as thy sword may have been." Pressing hard to remind Washington of his unique

place in history, Pleasants begged "that thou may not
. . . sully in thy private retreat the honors thou hast
acquired in the field. Remember the cause for which
thou wert called to the command of the American
army—the cause of liberty and the rights of mankind." How would history remember Washington,
Pleasants asked, if "impartial thinking men" read
"that many who were warm advocates for that noble
cause . . . are now sitting down in a state of ease and
dissipation and extravagance on the labor of slaves"
and, after "the greatest fatigue and dangers in that
cause[,] should now withhold . . . the right of freedom [that] is acknowledged to be the natural and
unalienable right of all mankind?" In a final prick
to Washington's conscience, Pleasants warned: "How
inconsistent . . . will it appear to posterity should it
be recorded that the great General Washington . . .
[had] been instrumental in relieving those states
from tyranny and oppression yet . . . continued those
evils as to keep a number of people in slavery who by
nature are equally entitled to freedom as himself."[42]

So far as we know, Washington did not answer
Pleasants's letter, perhaps because he had given up
the idea of joining Lafayette's experiment. Lafayette
by this time had purchased an estate in French Guiana and was settling his slaves there with promises of

freedom. Writing from Mount Vernon in May 1786, Washington showed signs of waffling. Dismayed, Lafayette wrote: "I would never have drawn my sword in the cause of America if I could have conceived thereby that I was founding a land of slavery." Rather than blaming his own change of heart about whether to free his slaves, Washington blamed "the minds of the people of this country," who would not tolerate Lafayette's "benevolence" and "humanity." Contrary to Madison's report that "sundry respectable persons" had argued on behalf of the Methodist petition for a gradual abolition act, Washington claimed that it "could scarcely obtain a reading."[43]

Yet slaveholding gnawed at Washington after he became the nation's first president in 1790. Wiencek has found evidence that Washington drafted a public statement in which he would announce as he assumed the presidency that he was freeing some of his slaves and preparing others for eventual emancipation. Had this occurred, it would have established the precedent that the man elected to the highest office in the new republic should disavow slavery before taking office. The ripple effect might have been enormous. Wiencek explains that Washington had "experienced a moral epiphany" and did not, in the early 1790s, believe that the obstacles to emancipation set forth by Lower South politicians were "insuperable to him at all." Washington drew back from this breathtaking action, but early in his second presidential term he told his private secretary, Tobias Lear, of his hope "to liberate a certain species of property which I possess, very repugnantly to my own feelings."[44]

Near at hand, only a short distance from Mount Vernon, occurred an event that presented Washington with another chance to turn pangs of conscience into concrete action. His neighbor Robert Carter III, whose family name was synonymous with Virginia slaveowning power, astonished the state's aristocracy in 1791 by penning a deed of gift that would free all of his 509 slaves, who worked over fifteen thousand acres of land on fourteen separate plantations. Carter might have been dismissed as eccentric, or as dazed by evangelical visions of the approaching millennium among the poor and often black parishioners at the small Baptist church he had joined, or as simply deranged. But his words were those that Washington and many of his fellow planters had already found unexceptional: "I have for some time past," wrote Carter, "been convinced that to retain them in slavery is contrary to the true principles of religion and justice." Where Carter differed from his neighbors was the logical completion of this sentence: "and that therefore it was my duty to manumit them." Carter began releasing slaves in groups and set them up on land of their own, sometimes within sight of Nomini Hall, his Potomac River plantation seat. He invited them to rename themselves in a kind of symbolic rebirth, and he repulsed attempts of white neighbors to contest his deed of gift. Through this self-sacrificing act, demonstrating that emancipation was not impossible but a matter of choice, Carter provided a model for other powerful men to follow. Many did follow—to the extent that one of every eight black Virginians was free by the year of Washington's death, 1799.[45]

Five years after Carter's deed of gift, in 1796, two men known intimately to Washington provided the president with another opportunity to make a crucial difference on an issue he declared was dear to his heart. Richard Randolph, scion of a socially prominent and wealthy Virginia family and cousin of Jefferson, wrote a will providing for the emancipation of all the slaves he inherited from his famous father, John Randolph. Richard's father had died when the boy was five years old, and the man his widowed mother married was St. George Tucker. Mentored by George Wythe and deeply influenced by his stepfather, Randolph penned his will at age twenty-five and filled it with castigations of slaveowners who "exercised the most lawless and monstrous tyranny" over African people "in contradiction to their own declaration of rights."[46] To ensure they had a chance to enjoy their freedom, Randolph provided four hundred acres of his land to be given to them as their own.

Almost simultaneously, Richard Randolph's stepfather, St. George Tucker, presented his abolition plan to the Virginia legislature, only months before Washington would retire from the presidency. But Washington again would not make any public statement against slavery. "Nobody," complained Tucker bitterly, "was prepared to meet the blind fury of the enemies of freedom" in Virginia.[47] A leader of men under arms, Washington could not bring himself to become a leader of unarmed men appealing to the nation's conscience.

The Virginian who, next to Washington, had the greatest moral capital and political influence to trade on also spurned the opportunity to help end the system of coerced labor, though he knew it compromised the American republic that he believed would be a model for all nations to emulate. By the early 1790s Jefferson had become an international symbol, "identified in the public mind," both at home and abroad, as his biographer Dumas Malone writes, "with the freedom of individual human beings from political tyranny and oppression of any sort." No founding father was blunter about the loathsomeness of slavery. Jefferson called it "an abominable crime," "a hideous blot" on civilized society, a "moral and political depravity." Moreover, Jefferson possessed the kind of mind that could have made the difference: "a restless, tenacious mind," according to Bernard Bailyn, "as fertile in formulating abstract ideas as in solving the most ordinary, mundane problems," and in which "through it all there glows a humane and generous purpose: to . . . meliorate the condition of life; to broaden the reach of liberty; and to assist in the pursuit of happiness."[48]

But Jefferson brought none of these qualities to bear on the issue of slavery. "Only against slavery did he appear paralyzed in policy and immobilized even in imagination," notes Michael Zuckerman. Jefferson squandered the respect he enjoyed as a national leader and an internationally famous son of the Enlightenment. It was this paralysis of will that led William Lloyd Garrison, after Jefferson's death, to remark that, if Jefferson had freed all, or many, of his slaves, "what an all-conquering influence must have attended his illustrious example!"[49] In his attachment to never-ending renovations at Monticello, Jefferson buried the thought of giving freedom to the hundreds of slaves laboring for him there.[50] In 1817, nine years before he died, he refused to free some of his slaves even when he had an opportunity to receive full compensation for them. Almost two decades before, he had pledged to his friend General Thaddeus Kosciuszko, the Polish military engineer who had fought in the American Revolution and whom he called the "truest son of liberty" he knew, to serve as executor of Kosciuszko's will. In the will, Kosciuszko, who died in 1817, provided that his estate, about $17,000, should be used to free as many of the slaves at Monticello as the money would purchase. Rather than serve as executor, however, Jefferson had the estate put into probate, where it remained in the federal courts until 1852. At $200 per slave, an average price Jefferson himself estimated in 1824, he could have freed more than 80 of the approximately 230 slaves he owned at the time. At his death, Jefferson left so many debts that all but 5 of his slaves were sold at auction to satisfy his creditors.[51]

Aside from the lives of his own slaves, the larger matter was statesmanship. Dumas Malone, allowing that Jefferson's influence was mainly exerted through private letters, calls him "one of the most effective party leaders in our history." This was certainly the case when Jefferson drafted the Ordinance of 1784, which included the pregnant wording: "After the year 1800 . . . there shall be neither slavery nor involuntary servitude in any of the . . . states" created out of the western domain. This bold stroke against slavery, for which Jefferson was willing to invest some of his political capital, obtained the approval of six states in the Continental Congress and lost the necessary seventh state, New Jersey, because a delegate was sick and absent.[52] Jefferson's outspokenness on slavery thereafter began to evaporate. Roger Kennedy opines that Jefferson's "tragedy lay in his unwillingness to make full use of his talent for persuasion to tip the balance when, on a series of occasions, choices were made to permit, and sometimes to encourage, the spread of slavery." Joyce Appleby concurs that Jefferson "backed away from attacking the institution as his power to do something about it increased." David Brion Davis points out that from this time Jefferson justified inaction on the slavery issue on the distinctly un-Jeffersonian grounds that the slaves and their abolitionist friends must "await with patience the workings of an overruling providence, and hope that that is preparing deliverance of these our suffering brethren." What could the nation's emerging young leaders, who by Jefferson's own account were embracing abolitionism, think, asks Davis, when they heard their intellectual model "recommending faith in providence as a substitute for social action? . . . If the great Father of Democracy had refrained from giving public voice to his convictions, how could lesser men presume superior wisdom?"[53]

Jefferson remained utterly silent, both publicly and privately, first as Kentucky debated its constitution and second after the Louisiana Purchase of 1803. "One might have expected the author of the Ordinance of 1784," writes Don Fehrenbacher, "to view the acquisition as a tabula rasa and make some effort to inhibit the spread of the institution [of slavery] into a vast domain still largely free of white settlement." But "Jefferson as president never lifted his land against slavery, except in the matter of terminating the importation of slaves." Instead, "Jefferson's administration," now "functionally proslavery," produced a "rigorous slave code" to be used by Congress in organizing the new Louisiana Territory.[54]

Historians often explain Jefferson's refusal to work to prevent the spread of slavery as the nation expanded by the fact that his main political support came from the South. Yet Jefferson knew he never would have occupied the Presidential Mansion with-

out an electoral victory in New York and a split electoral vote in Pennsylvania. After a Federalist senator
from Connecticut put forward an amendment to the
Louisiana Territory legislation that would have freed
male slaves by their twenty-second birthday and female slaves by their nineteenth, the House of Representatives passed the amendment but the Senate
voted it down seventeen to eleven. In a move that
would have gained him international acclaim and an
indelible mark in history, Jefferson might have altered the outcome, which opened the West to slavery.[55]

In a torrent of Jeffersonian studies in recent years,
much has been said about how Jefferson was hobbled
in his professed desire to free his slaves by his view of
people of African descent as indelibly inferior. This, it
is argued, tainted all his thoughts about repairing
the Achilles' heel of the new republic. Jefferson could
not imagine white and black people living together in
freedom—or so he said, though for most of his life
he lived at Monticello surrounded by black people,
some of them related to him through his father-in-
law's miscegenation, some through his own liaison
with Sally Hemings. Africans were "inferior to the
whites in . . . mind and body," he contended, because
they were "originally a distinct race, or made distinct

111

by time and circumstances." If that was so, he reasoned, "nothing is more certainly written in the book
of fate than that the two races, equally free, cannot
live in the same government."[56]

Some historians today argue that Jefferson did not
actually believe in this doctrine of inherent black inferiority but instead used it to shield himself from
charges of gross duplicity. David Grimsted, for example, wastes no words in calling Jefferson's racial theo-
rizing "obvious self-serving hypocrisy," a pseudo-the-
ory advanced "to palliate the brutal exclusions from
all civil and most human rights of those blacks that
so contributed to his and his society's convenience."
John C. Miller opines that Jefferson created "a protec-
tive device" by spinning a web of make-believe—con-
veying the impression that "slavery had been placed
in the course of ultimate extinguishment," often
speaking "as though the event had already occurred."
This relieved him "of the overpowering, paralyzing
sense of guilt" and "tended to diminish the need for
the kind of incessant, dedicated, and uncompromising action that had distinguished Jefferson's career as
a revolutionary."[57]

Whether or not Jefferson spun out his ideas of
innate black inferiority to justify the waning of his
commitment to the abolition of slavery, it is certain

that he wounded the abolitionist cause by holding up for ridicule the examples of black genius that had appeared in the revolutionary era—cases that contradicted his notion of innate inferiority. Reading Phillis Wheatley's poetry, he diminished her talent with an almost perverse enthusiasm. "Religion indeed has produced a Phillis Wheatley," he wrote in his *Notes on the State of Virginia,* published in the year of Wheatley's death, "but it could not produce a poet." Such a dismissal brought refutations from many quarters. Samuel Stanhope Smith, about to become president of the College of New Jersey, asked how many southern planters "could have written poems equal to those of P. Whateley?" The Kentuckian and continental army veteran Gilbert Imlay, lover of the feminist writer Mary Wollstonecraft, described Jefferson's theory of inborn racial inferiority as "disgraceful" and "paltry sophistry and nonsense" and asked about Wheatley, "What white person on this continent has written more beautiful lines?" Wheatley's poems reached all the way to Goettingen University, where Johann Friedrich Blumenbach, the world-famous founder of comparative anatomy who found no physiological evidence of black inequality, spoke in praise of her.[58]

Likewise, Jefferson sneered at Benjamin Banneker's use of spheroid trigonometry to create published and widely read almanacs charting the movement of the heavenly bodies. The nation's best astronomer, David Rittenhouse of Philadelphia, thought Banneker's first almanac a "very extraordinary performance." But Jefferson airily dismissed Banneker with a comment that he "had a mind of very common stature indeed."[59]

Whether a deeply held prejudice or self-serving hypocrisy, Jefferson's ideas of the innate inferiority of people of African descent led him to dark warnings about racial intermingling. Freed slaves, he insisted in his *Notes on Virginia,* must be "removed beyond the reach of mixture." If abolishing slavery became the national policy, then a stable biracial or mixed-race republic would be an impossibility. Why such an "aversion . . . to the mixture of color," as Jefferson himself expressed it? It is all the more puzzling since Jefferson, as has been known since his own day (and recently confirmed by DNA analysis), maintained a long intimate relationship with his light-skinned slave Sally Hemings, who was the half-sister of Jefferson's deceased wife (her father was Jefferson's father-in-law). In his personal life, Jefferson was not allergic to what he publicly condemned. Claiming that freed slaves were "as incapable as children of taking care

Benjamin Banneker. Engraving from *Benjamin Bannaker's Pennsylvania, Delaware, Maryland, and Virginia Almanac for the Year of Our Lord 1795*. Houghton Library, Harvard University.

In spite of his mathematical, surveying, and instrument-making skills, Benjamin Banneker made only a modest impression on Thomas Jefferson. Reluctant to acknowledge innate African intellectuality, Jefferson did not know quite what to make of Banneker.

of themselves," he held fast to the view that child-ish freedmen would insist on complete equality and that equality would lead to a mixing of the races. This would pollute Anglo-Saxon blood, pull white in-tellectual superiority down to the level of inferior Af-ricans, and eventually destroy the national genius. Consistent with this view, Jefferson attempted in the early 1790s to banish white Virginia women (but not black women) who bore "mulatto" children, defined by the state in 1792 as anyone "who shall have one-fourth part or more of Negro blood." This was pa-tently an attempt to police the sexual activities of white women who chose black consorts, while at the same time maintaining white men's access to black women. "The world's leading democratic spokes-man," comments Grimsted, had emerged as the "world's preeminent racist theorist."[60]

Nothing could better express the dismay of black Americans with Jefferson's moral retreat than the words of Benjamin Banneker. In 1791, when Banneker was in his fifties, he implored Jefferson to rethink his views about African inferiority and chided him for continuing to hold slaves at Monticello and his other plantations: "I apprehend you will embrace every op-portunity to eradicate that train of absurd and false ideas and opinions which so generally prevail with respect to us, and that your sentiments are concurrent with mine, which are that one universal father hath given being to us all and that he hath not only made us all of one flesh but that he hath also without partiality afforded us all the same sensations, and endowed us all with the same faculties." Reminding Jefferson of his oft-quoted words in the preamble of the Declaration of Independence that "all men are created equal and that they are endowed by their creator with certain unalienable rights," Banneker rebuked Jefferson for "detaining by fraud and violence so numerous a part of my brethren under groaning captivity and cruel oppression." Should not Jefferson "be found guilty of that most criminal act, which you professedly detested in others"?[61]

Henry Adams, a grandson of John Adams, put his finger on Jefferson's massive inconsistency and failure of leadership: "His yearning for sympathy"—that is, sympathy from white Virginia men of wealth and power—"was almost feminine." Dumas Malone agrees: "He wanted to be liked, or, to be more precise, he hated to be disliked." Avoiding conflict with white friends and compatriots kept Jefferson from helping to avert the holocaust that he knew, to his final days, was coming closer and closer.[62]

As for Madison, in his case a towering intellect did

not translate into political leadership, either in the crucial 1780s and 1790s or later as the nation's fourth president. As principal drafter of the Constitution and the Bill of Rights, Madison indisputably had enormous moral and political credit to draw upon. Nor is there doubt that, in Drew McCoy's words, his "antislavery credentials can be fairly described as impeccable." In Philadelphia at the end of the Revolutionary War, Madison had agreed that his runaway slave Billy was "merely . . . coveting that liberty for which we have paid the price of so much blood, and have proclaimed so often to be the right . . . of every human being." Like Washington, Madison had toyed in the 1780s with the thought of extricating himself from slave-based Virginia by buying land in upstate New York, where he might become a gentleman farmer using free labor. He abandoned this plan, but "throughout a long public career (and an even longer life) he never wavered for a moment in utterly condemning the institution. His categorical opposition to slavery generated an unyielding commitment to abolishing it in the United States. For him, the question was never if, but rather when and how." Yet Madison, like Jefferson and Washington, shrank from becoming an active part of the "how."[63]

Tellingly, in the 1790s Madison penned an essay, "The Influence of Domestic Slavery on Government," in which he warned that southern slave regimes could not help producing concentrations of political power—aristocracies was the proper name for them—that ran squarely athwart the democratic foundations on which the republic was built. But Madison kept this essay to himself, withholding it from other essays he published in the *National Gazette* in the early 1790s to mobilize opposition to the Federalist policies engineered by Alexander Hamilton. "His political career," writes McCoy, "became no less dependent on evading the implications of the political analysis that he had committed to his notebook in the early 1790s." Later in his career, Madison grew stronger in his belief that the American Revolution represented "a decisive turning point in human history," one that would teach other nations that the future lay in instituting self-governing republics. Stitched to this belief was Madison's certainty that a newborn republic could not survive the stain of slavery and that America's international influence would always be vitiated by slavery's continuation. But for all his private anguish, Madison could not move from word to deed any more than Washington or Jefferson. "Why," asks

McCoy, "didn't this sage and honest statesman understand—and publicly acknowledge—the need for
swift and effective action against slavery?"[64]

Answering that question did not trouble historians until recent years because the question itself had
not been asked. But in recent times scholars have
reached for answers, though they have been hobbled
by a desire to embrace the founding fathers as presenting America's better self. For moral philosophers
the answer has resided in the realm of character
weakness of the sort that everyone from the Greek
dramatists to Reinhold Niebuhr has made familiar.
From psychologists we gain some insight into the ca-
pacity of even finely honed minds to embrace contradictory propositions and tolerate even massive disso-
nance between what they say and what they do. For
political scientists and political historians men like
Jefferson, Washington, and Madison had to stay attuned to the brute fact that their political power
rested on popular approbation; and that even if they
were willing to sacrifice continued officeholding to
win the gratitude of posterity, they had to prioritize
issues and sharply limit their risk-taking.[65] In this
view, instead of lacking political courage, they prop-
erly exercised, or sadly lacked, political judgment in
calculating how they could trade on their national

and international fame to produce changes that in the long term would benefit the country and fulfill its founding principles.

Historians are not mathematicians, and even if they were, they could not calculate with precision the degrees to which moral, psychological, economic, or political elements contributed to the failure of the founding fathers to become risk takers rather than risk averters on the matter of slavery. But the result is painfully evident. If Washington had carried through with his pledge in 1783 to join Lafayette in "the grand experiment" of freeing their slaves, if Jefferson, Madison, and a few other luminous Virginians who professed to despise slavery had stepped forward to support the Methodists' appeal to the Virginia legislature in 1785, or to follow the example of Robert Carter III and Richard Randolph in emancipating their slaves, or to endorse or improve one of the gradual emancipation plans put forward by Virginia's most eminent jurists, and if northern leaders such as John Adams and Benjamin Franklin had drawn fully on their fund of respect to support a plan for gradual emancipation and convince northerners of their obligation to contribute to its implementation for the sake of an enduring union, the course of history might have changed. Sixty years after Jefferson became president in 1801, the bloodletting began that would claim the lives of more than six hundred thousand Americans and shatter the bodies of as many more, in a war in which emancipation became one of the Union's main goals. Roughly one lay dead and another crippled for each of the slaves consigned to perpetual unpaid labor in the new United States as Jefferson took office as the nation's third president.

# 3

## RACE AND CITIZENSHIP
## IN THE EARLY REPUBLIC

GEORGE WASHINGTON'S DEATH in 1799 triggered an outpouring of adulation for the "father of his country" and soon brought the remarkable news that in his will he provided for the freedom of his 146 slaves. The dower slaves his wife had brought into the marriage were legally beyond his reach, but by freeing the slaves over whom he had control he offered another opportunity for powerful political leaders such as Jefferson and Madison to return to the purity of the founding documents. But nearly the opposite occurred. The year 1800 brought Jefferson's presidential victory over John Adams, ushering in a four-decade era when Jeffersonians dominated the executive and legislative branches of government. Though regarded as the party of the common people, dedicated to broadening the franchise, relaxing the restrictions on immigrants seeking naturalization, and restoring a state-centered republic, the Democratic-

Republicans also "extended the domain of white supremacy." "The Virginia Republican dynasty," Rogers
Smith tells us, redefined citizenship laws that eroded
the rights of African Americans and, as time went
on in the first quarter of the nineteenth century, even
denied that free people of color were citizens at all.
After 1800, "citizenship laws increasingly reflected
Jeffersonian views of American nationality," leaving
the Federalists (who have become in the historical
literature the party of the elite) as the main defend-
ers of black citizenship rights.[1] Thus, a state-centered
republic rendered itself largely incapable of solving
what was not a *state* problem but a *national* problem.
The stage was being set for the creation of the killing
fields through which Americans of all regions, all colors, and all dispositions would walk two generations
later.

The political and ideological journeys of two Philadelphians, one black, the other white—both young
men of the revolutionary era and longtime residents
of the city known as the capital of American benevolence and Enlightenment idealism—neatly represent
the argument that reverberated throughout the nation in the first quarter of the nineteenth century
about the matter of race and citizenship in the early
republic. The African American was James Forten,

Philadelphia's most successful black businessman up to his death in 1842. His five published letters to the public in 1813 and his subsequent writings tell us much about how black northerners were thinking about citizenship in the critical period leading up to the Missouri Compromise of 1820, Denmark Vesey's plot in 1822, and the publication of David Walker's *Appeal to the Coloured Citizens of the World* in 1829. The white Philadelphian was Tench Coxe, at first a shrewd Federalist merchant and then a longtime Jeffersonian officeholder and leading political economist. While living only a few blocks from Forten, he published two sets of essays, one in 1809, the other in the winter of 1820–21. In these essays Coxe provided a figurative road map that most white Americans followed in redefining citizenship and national identity in the period when an irreparable national fissure began to appear.

James Forten thought of himself as thoroughly American from an early age. Only as he matured and became successful did he think of himself as African American. In time, he came to wonder whether being African American would allow those of dark skin to be American at all. Born in 1766, the grandson of an African who was one of the first enslaved Pennsylvanians to gain his freedom, Forten learned to read and

write at the Quakers' African School, and he was influenced as well by Anthony Benezet, Philadelphia's
Quaker reformer who devoted himself to teaching
the children of the poor. Forten's father died when
the boy was seven. He was eleven when the British-
officered regiment of Black Guides and Pioneers,
composed of escaped Virginia slaves who responded
to Dunmore's Proclamation, occupied Philadelphia
in the winter of 1777–78. Forten and his mother
no doubt knew what the German Lutheran minister Henry Muhlenberg reported: that Pennsylvania's
slaves "secretly wished that the British army might
win, for then all Negro slaves will gain their freedom."[2] The flight of many of the city's slaves to the
British, along with a number of free blacks, could
hardly have gone unnoticed by the adolescent Forten.

But the young Forten would have none of this.
Perhaps gaining his optimistic outlook from his free
parents, and perhaps convinced from Benezet's lessons that Africans were no different from whites in
their potential, James—at age fifteen—signed on as a
powder boy on Stephen Decatur's 22-gun *Royal Louis*.
Thus began a heroic career. For years Philadelphians
told of how Forten was the only survivor at his gun
station when Decatur's ship dueled with a British
warship in 1781; how he was captured on the next voy-

James Forten, watercolor. Historical Society of
Pennsylvania (HSP), Leon Gardiner Collection.

The artist who portrayed James Forten is unknown (and it
is only informed speculation that has led historians to
identify the sitter as Forten). The painter may have been
the young Philadelphian Robert Douglass Jr., who in 1834
exhibited a "Portrait of a Gentleman" at the Pennsylvania
Academy of the Arts. Two years earlier Douglass had
created a huge transparency of Washington Crossing the
Delaware that was displayed at the State House (now
Independence Hall) as part of the celebration of the
centennial of Washington's birth.

age and spurned an offer from a British captain to take him to England, as his son's companion, where he could pursue a satisfactory career; how he told the British captain "No, No! I am here a prisoner for the liberties of my country; I never, NEVER, shall prove a traitor to her interests"; how he was clapped into a rotting British prison ship in New York harbor and gave up a chance to be smuggled out in a trunk of clothes; how he walked barefoot from New York to Philadelphia in 1783 after the British released their American prisoners; and how, after the war, he became a valued sailmaker in the employ of Robert Bridges. When the white sailmaker retired in 1798, he handed over his sail loft to Forten.[3]

Forten imagined that the revolutionary generation's rhetoric of natural rights would usher in a biracial democracy in Pennsylvania and create a nation where colorblind national identity flowed from an allegiance to the nation and the state. Why not? He had fought bravely in the American Revolution; was a pillar of St. Thomas African Episcopal church, one of two black churches founded in Philadelphia in 1793; succeeded as artisan and businessman who employed interracial crew of thirty sailmakers; owned a home where some of his neighbors were eminent Philadelphians; counted white merchants among his friends; and was a confidant of Paul Cuffe, the New Bedford Afro-Indian shipbuilder, merchant, and ship captain who sailed the deep blue seas all the way to Africa. Moreover, Forten held before him the preamble of the Pennsylvania Constitution of 1776, assuring him that, if the revolutionary generation remained true to its words, the doctrine of human equality would be the future. "All men," it read, "are born equally free and independent, and have certain natural, inherent, and inalienable rights." The preamble of Pennsylvania's gradual abolition act of 1780 also affirmed the unitary nature of humankind, what the legislators called a "universal civilization": "It is not for us to enquire why, in the creation of mankind, the inhabitants of the several parts of the world were distinguished by a difference in feature or complexion. It is sufficient to know that all are the work of an Almighty Hand . . . who placed them in their various situations [and] hath extended equally his care and protection to all." Forten believed in what a modern scholar of citizenship has claimed was the general presumption of the post-revolutionary period—"that membership [in civil society] was acquired automatically by all those born under the Republic."[4]

But Forten's faith that white Pennsylvanians

would honor these commitments was wearing thin by the early years of Jefferson's presidency. Like most black and some white Philadelphians, Forten took satisfaction in the slave rebellion in Saint Domingue (to become Haiti), which began in 1791 and ultimately overthrew the brutal French slave regime and established the first black republic in the Americas. But he also had to take the measure of the fear of many white northerners, and of almost all white southerners, that the news from Saint Domingue would spread black rebellion all over America.[5] Forten knew that refugees from southern slavery, filtering into Philadelphia, caused white resentment, and that Irish immigrants in the 1790s competed uneasily with free black people for bottom-rung jobs. He watched uneasily as Congress rejected petitions from black Philadelphians and the Pennsylvania Abolition Society to rescind the hated Fugitive Slave Act of 1793 and abolish the still-flourishing slave trade.[6]

If the rise of racial hostility in the City of Brotherly Love shook Forten's belief in one American peoplehood, he was more distressed by an outbreak of racial rancor on July 4 in about 1804 that struck at the notion of free black birthright citizenship. For years, Philadelphians of all classes and colors had gathered in the square facing Independence Hall, where the nation's birth certificate had been signed, to listen to speeches about the blessings of liberty and the prospects for national greatness. But this time, sullen whites drove free black citizens from the festivities with a torrent of curses. At this moment James Forten's political awakening occurred, perhaps also spurred by Congress's failure in 1804 to pass a bill that would free male slaves by their twenty-second birthday and female slaves by their nineteenth, a measure supported by many northern Jeffersonians.[7] The worsening situation on the ground in Philadelphia sickened Forten. Black Philadelphians, he wrote, "dare not be seen after twelve o'clock in the day, upon the field to enjoy the times" without fearing assault from whites "like the destroying Hyena or the avaricious Wolf." In allowing white toughs to control public spaces in the city and to drive black Philadelphians from the celebration of nationhood, white political leaders and municipal authorities implicitly renounced the idea that citizenship was the entitlement of all free people regardless of color. "Is it not wonderful," Forten exclaimed sarcastically, "that the day set apart for the festival of liberty, should be abused by the advocates of freedom, in endeavoring to sully what they profess to adore?"[8]

Forten's alarm increased as the Pennsylvania legislature began considering bills in 1804 to seal the state off from incoming black migrants, to impose a special tax on black householders for the support of the poor of their color, to require all free black adults to carry freedom certificates, to sentence those failing to produce a certificate, without jury trial, to seven years imprisonment, and to sell into slavery any black person convicted of a property crime in order to compensate the victim. Each of these provisions directly assaulted the principle that citizenship conferred fundamental privileges and immunities without distinction of color. For nine years such bills failed in the legislature, but in 1813, when the mayor and city councilmen of Philadelphia supported such bills, Forten took up his pen. "Search the legends of tyranny and find no precedent," he thundered in five published letters. "It has been left for Pennsylvania to raise her ponderous arm against the liberties of the black, whose greatest boast has been that he resided in a state where civil liberty and sacred justice were administered alike to all."[9]

What had happened to the revolutionary vision of unalienable rights? When the founding fathers and the writers of Pennsylvania's constitution said "all men are created equal," did they mean only white men (as many historians have asserted ever since)?

Forten denied this emphatically. "This idea [of natural rights]," he affirmed, "embraces the Indian and the European, the Savage and the Saint, the Peruvian and the Laplander, the white Man and the African, and whatever measures are adopted subversive of this inestimable privilege, are in direct violation of the letter and spirit of our Constitution, and become subject to the animadversion of all, particularly those who are deeply interested in the measure." The legislative bills, Forten cried, would convert the center of American benevolence into a center of repression: "The story will fly from the north to the south, and the advocates of slavery, the traders in human blood, will smile contemptuously at the once boasted moderation and humanity of Pennsylvania!" And where, he asked, would slaves emancipated in the South go? "Shut every state against him, and, like Pharaoh's kine, drive him into the sea.—Is there no spot on earth that will protect him? Against their inclination, his ancestors were forced from their homes by traders in human flesh, and even under such circumstances the wretched offspring are denied the protection you afford to brutes."[10]

Forten's incandescent rhetoric about universal rights and his attempt to hold back the rising tide of race-based legislation in the early nineteenth century made him the most important free black voice in the nation as the War of 1812 unfolded. More than black clergymen, who at this time were the principal spokesmen of their communities and nearly the only black men who could put the printed word before the public, Forten challenged white power with a sharp wit and clarity of expression. "Has the GOD who made the white man and the black," he asked, "left any record declaring us a different species? Are we not sustained by the same power, supported by the same food, hurt by the same wounds, wounded by the same wrongs, pleased with the same delights, and propagated by the same means. And should we not then enjoy the same liberty, and be protected by the same laws." Forten knew many of the authors of Pennsylvania's constitution, and he now reminded the white legislators that these revolutionary architects "felt that they had no more authority to enslave us, than England had to tyrannize over them . . . Actuated by these sentiments they adopted the glorious fabrick of our liberties, and, declaring 'all men' free, they did not particularize white and black, because they never supposed it would be made a question whether *we were men or not.*"[11]

Forten's letters to the public—meant to appeal to the conscience of the state's legislators—may have carried weight. In any case, the legislature in 1813 drew back from patently discriminatory laws aimed at free black Pennsylvanians and former southern slaves seeking a new life in Pennsylvania. It was an important victory. But it could not stop the juggernaut of white racial hostility bearing down on free black communities and threatening to pulverize the concept of colorblind citizenship.[12]

At first Tench Coxe, Forten's neighbor, was not part of that juggernaut, but in a few years he began providing a rationale for it. Coxe commanded much respect as one of the most distinguished writers of his generation on American manufacturing, commerce, and political economy. After it reorganized in 1787, the Pennsylvania Abolition Society (PAS) was pleased to persuade Coxe to become its secretary, for this gave the organization new breadth and respect. In 1790 Coxe joined two Quaker PAS leaders to draft the society's first petition to Congress to halt the slave trade.[13] By 1796 Coxe moved from the Federalist party to the Jeffersonian camp; thereafter he became a Jeffersonian political lieutenant and officeholder. All the while, he thought deeply about how the American character had come to be distinctive and how the new republic should define citizenship.

Coxe's first public comments on this appeared in a

series of essays penned in 1809 under the title "The New World: An Enquiry into the National Character of the People of the United States of America." Here he spun out a thesis about American uniqueness—one that James Forten might well have endorsed. Lacing his essays with references to freedom and oppression, Coxe pictured the Americans as a band of Crusoes who had banished tyranny and ushered in a heroic age of liberty. Greatly to their credit, the Americans had molded "a perfect civil uniformity, unknown and impracticable in any other maritime empire and highly influential upon the uniformity of the national character." Consistent with his earlier support for the Pennsylvania Abolition Society, Coxe continued that "the white and free black inhabitants are all included in this observation; for it is a truth, that the free blacks regularly adopt and display the institutions, apparel, furniture, and habits of the whites. They are generally Episcopalians, Calvinists, and Methodists in those places where all the Christian sects are within their free observation."[14]

Now Coxe nailed down his belief in a single human race: "*Man* is justly contemplated, by our laws and by our political science, as an intelligent creation of the divine power. It is known that the highest intellect of the red and black races of men is sensibly better than that of the feeblest of the whites." From this fundamental belief flowed the notion of an un-racialized citizenship. "As we cannot discriminate *as to rights* among the whites by the principle of intellect," wrote Coxe, "the same rule presses itself upon our regard with respect to the free people of the red and black races. Divine providence has ordained the existence of the coloured races of men, and we believe and know, that the same supreme authority has imperiously ordained humanity and justice among his intelligent and responsible creatures. Our institutions, therefore, consider all men alike." Here was a liberal position that veered from the Jeffersonian drift toward what Rogers Smith has called "a racially coded system of citizenship and half-citizenship."[15]

If Forten was pleased in 1809 with Coxe's treatise on the universality of humankind and his insistence that the nation's civil institutions applied to free blacks as well as whites, the black sailmaker had much to be concerned about in what was issuing from other quarters in Philadelphia. Men of science also began discussing American character, race, and citizenship and were reaching foreboding conclusions. In a full-scale attack on the environmentalist theory that since the Revolution had dominated thinking about racial differences, mid-Atlantic scientific thinkers now began avowing that irreparable deficiencies in moral and religious reasoning rendered large numbers of Americans useless as part of the nation's citizenry. Leading the way was Charles Caldwell, who had studied medicine at the University of Pennsylvania under Benjamin Rush, Philadelphia's leading white supporter of African American progress. In two long essays Caldwell tried to dismantle the environmentalist explanation that black deficiencies were the result of lifetimes under brutalizing slavery.[16] Foreshadowing the rise of the racist antebellum school of anthropology in the United States, Caldwell published his "Essay on the Causes of the Variety of Complexion and Figure in the Human Species" in 1811 and in 1814 followed with a similar essay arguing that differences between races were innate and thus completely resistant to environmental modification.[17] Caldwell's assertions of the inherent inferiority of Africans and their descendants, a descent into what a recent historian calls "irrationalism and narcissistic raptures over whiteness," nearly coincided with Rush's death in 1813 as if to punctuate the fact that one chapter of race relations in Philadelphia was ending and another beginning.[18] This was the vanguard *poly*genesis theory developed fully in the 1830s by Samuel George Morton, another Philadelphian. The environmentalist line of argument that supported the notion of the indivisibility of the human species—expressed so passionately by James Forten in his 1813 *Letters from a Man of Colour*—was now on the defensive.[19]

Sociology had also entered the argument through the side door, also on the side of nationality and citizenship defined as strictly a white man's affair. Impinging on arguments about the origins of the human species—whether many or one—and on related arguments about a fused citizenry or a fissured civil society was a growing fear among white northerners in the early nineteenth century about the effects of emancipation on racial intermixture.

As Winthrop Jordan has argued, the belief was "nearly universal" among white Americans that the emancipation of slaves after the Revolution would "inevitably lead to racial intermixture" and that such intermingling would sadly prove "that civilized man had turned beast in the forest." There were a few exceptions to be sure. Most notable was Princeton's president in the 1790s, Samuel Stanhope Smith, who hoped that emancipated slaves would be settled on western lands where they would intermarry with whites. This, he reasoned, would "bring the two races nearer together, and, in a course of time, . . . obliterate those wide distinctions which are now created by diversity of complexion" and magnified "by prejudice." Also in the 1790s, Patrick Henry advocated Indian-white marriage and pushed Virginia to offer bounties for such mingling of blood. But Smith and Henry were distinctly minority voices, drowned out in the early nineteenth century by the belief that intermixture with blacks or Indians would stain white blood and that the purity of the nation itself would be fatally compromised. Thomas Jefferson's view, that the emancipated slave must "be removed beyond the reach of mixture" so that the black American would not corrupt "the blood of his master" was certainly the majority view among whites. In fact, it was one of the propelling sentiments behind all colonization schemes of the early republic. "Manifestly," writes Jordan, "America's destiny was white"—at least in the view of most whites.[20]

In the Philadelphia of Forten and Coxe, virulent opposition to interracial marriage surfaced well before the black sailmaker wrote his *Letters from a Man of Colour.* Reverend Nicholas Collin, the rector of Gloria Dei Church, where many black men and women had taken vows, refused to marry a black man and the white widow of a sea captain who came to him in the winter of 1794. For the next few years, Collin wrote disapprovingly in his marriage register of similar requests, remarking that he was "not willing to have blame from public opinion" for sanctioning mixed marriages. Six years later he fretted that "a particoloured race will soon make a great portion of the population in Philadelphia" in spite of "public opinion disapproving such wedlocks." Joseph Drinker, a Quaker leader, opposed granting full admission into the Society of Friends to Hannah Burrows, a light-skinned woman who attended meetings "as a preacher or teacher." If she gained membership, he reasoned, "the privilege of intermarriage with the whites," which he called "objectionable," "could not be withheld."[21]

Inherent in all such anxiety over interracial marriage was the notion that black blood would corrupt white blood. Such simmering fears came to a boil in 1806 in Philadelphia in the writings of Thomas Branagan, an avowed enemy of slavery. Of Irish Catholic background, Branagan had gone to sea at age thirteen, sailed on slave ships, supervised a slave plantation in Antigua, and landed on the shores of the Delaware River in 1799. By this time, he was thoroughly disgusted with slavery and began preaching in his self-learned manner to "the poor and needy, the halt, the maimed, and the blind." In *Preliminary*

*Essay on the Oppression of the Exiled Sons of Africa* (1804), Branagan spoke as vigorously against the inhumanity of slavery as the most erstwhile Quaker. But a year later, in *Serious Remonstrances Addressed to the Citizens of the Northern States* (1805), Branagan combined antislavery rhetoric with a heady brew of racism. He proposed to end "the contamination of the land which is sacred to liberty" by creating a black state in the newly acquired Louisiana Territory where the "poisonous fruit" of the tree of slavery should be shipped. Then, in dripping language revealing an obsession with interracial sex, Branagan painted a picture of black males swarming over "white women of easy virtue," hell-bent on obtaining white wives and producing "mungrels and mulattoes" so rapidly that "in the course of a few years . . . half the inhabitants of the city will be people of Colour." Equally ominous, Branagan, while promoting a federally established state for free black people, argued that they should not gain citizenship right but rather live out their lives as wards of the state. Coming just a year after he had defended black people as "sensible, ingenious, hospitable, and generous as any people, placed in such circumstances, and laboring under such disadvantages," Branagan's turnabout was stunning.[22]

The rising Negrophobia among ordinary white

Philadelphians and the strident writing of men such as Caldwell on the innate inferiority of Africans required Forten and other black leaders to reevaluate their situation and rethink their future. As in other northern cities, some free black Philadelphians began to think of themselves as a nation within a nation. If so, it made sense to create alternative celebrations of freedom, especially after their exclusion from white festivities on the Fourth of July. In Philadelphia (as in Boston), this began in 1808. January 1—marking the end of the slave trade and Haiti's independence day since 1804—became an African American day of commemoration, "the Day of Our Political Jubilee," as one black minister called it.[23] Now, black Philadelphians paraded and celebrated in their own way and on their own day. But they paraded as citizens, even though their entitlement to full citizenship was under attack.[24]

Historians have detected strains of black nationalism, or separatism, in the African American celebrations, yet the urban parades were generally "freedom festivals" meant to nurture an African American identity among people generally pursuing assimilationist ends in spite of spiraling racial antipathy. This desire to be fully American was apparent in Philadelphia during the War of 1812, when James Forten chaired a black Committee of Defense and led more than a thousand black men in 1814 out of the city to strengthen the Delaware River fortifications protecting Philadelphia from British naval attacks. If not permitted to shoulder guns, black men stepped forward eagerly with shovels to prove their patriotism and discharge their civic responsibility. Two years later, Philadelphia's Russell Parrott dwelt on how the black soldier had earned the rights of citizenship by fighting in the Revolution and War of 1812 "with noble daring, mingling his blood in the ungrateful soil that refused him everything but a grave."[25]

But the interclass and interracial harmony that prevailed in September 1814 when black and white shovel brigades stood shoulder to shoulder did not last. A year later, white Philadelphians, claiming to be bothered by the noise of emotional religious services, destroyed a black house of worship in the Northern Liberties. By this time, James Forten was reluctantly concluding that black Americans could achieve peoplehood and nationality only by becoming something other than Americans. That something would have to be outside the United States.

This, of course, was the position of the American Colonization Society, founded late in 1816, three years after Forten published his *Letters from a Man of*

*Colour.* A peculiar mixture of southerners and northerners, of pro-slavery and anti-slavery advocates, of
conservatives and liberals, the ACS proposed to pu-
rify the nation through the removal of dark-skinned
residents, in effect announcing that America was a
white man's republic.[26] Black Philadelphians such as
James Forten and Richard Allen at first believed that
emigrationism would be voluntary and occur on
black terms, not white. They would shortly change
their minds.

For black Philadelphians, the question of national
identity came to a dramatic head on a cold, wintry
night in January 1817. Believing themselves a part of a
biracial republic, not yet equal but progressing toward full citizenship, they flocked to a clamorous
meeting in the city's main black sanctuary, Richard
Allen's African Methodist Episcopal Church. Squeez-
ing his way forward to the pulpit, Forten marveled at
three thousand men packing the main floor, over-
flowing the U-shaped balcony, and spilling into the
street. Nearly three quarters of the city's black men
had gathered to speak their minds on citizenship and
national identity. Forten had been pondering the
meeting of white political leaders who three weeks
before in Washington had founded the ACS and issued statements that repatriating free black Ameri-

cans to Africa was the only solution to the nation's growing racial problem. Forten thought of his Rhode Island friend Paul Cuffe, the Afro-Indian ship captain who for more than a decade had been promoting resettlement in Africa, believing that black Americans had no future in the United States.[27]

So Forten, chairing the meeting, rose to address a sea of dark faces. The man who had staked his identity as an American and had prospered in the city of his birth called on Philadelphia's three notable black ministers—Richard Allen, Absalom Jones, and John Gloucester. All spelled out the advantages of returning to ancestral homelands. Then Forten endorsed the idea, reluctantly admitting that black Americans "will never become a people until they come out from amongst the white people." Now came time for a straw vote. Forten called first for the "ayes," those favoring a return to Africa. Not a voice was heard nor a hand lifted. Then he called for those opposed to this. One tremendous "no" arose, Forten later wrote, "as if it would bring down the walls of the building . . . There was not a soul that was in favor of going to Africa."[28]

The emotional meeting at Richard Allen's church in 1817, repeated throughout the nation over the next few years, had an annealing effect among black Americans. The black masses instinctively understood what some of their leaders did not—that while some white ACS leaders were sincere about helping black Americans and others were zealous to send black Christian missionaries to convert all Africans to Christianity, the colonization scheme was mostly the instrument of southerners whose main interest was a massive deportation of free blacks while providing cover for slavery's expansion.

Forten, Allen, and other black leaders in Philadelphia would dabble in colonization schemes in Canada and Haiti in the future, but never again would they speak on behalf of repatriation to Africa. The unanimously endorsed resolution presented after the vote taken at Richard Allen's church expressed a new commitment to abolitionism and racial equality. "Whereas our ancestors (not of choice) were the first successful cultivators of the wilds of America," the resolution affirmed, "we their descendants feel ourselves entitled to participate in the blessings of her luxuriant soil which their blood and sweat manured." Again referring to the founding documents on which common citizenship was based, black Philadelphians avowed "that any measure . . . having the tendency to banish us from her bosom, would not only be cruel, but in direct violation of those principles which have been the boast of the republic."[29]

Local supporters of the American Colonization Society still retained hope to win black northerners over to the idea of returning to Africa and in this way render moot the entire matter of black citizenship rights. In mid-1818, a Philadelphia newspaper printed a *faux* debate between William Penn (dead for almost a century), the recently deceased Absalom Jones, founder and minister of Philadelphia's St. Thomas African Episcopal Church; and Paul Cuffe, James Forten's friend who supported colonization of free black Americans to Sierra Leone. In the "dialogues on the African colony," Jones rejected repatriation as a deportation scheme designed to smother the efforts of abolitionists. Cuffe tried to convince him otherwise, and Penn, having consulted George Washington (also dead since 1799), reported that the founding father greatly favored the return to Africa for the good of black Americans. Finally, Absalom Jones swallowed his doubts that whatever pleased slavemasters could benefit free blacks. "My objections have been refuted," he said in this mock debate; "my scruples vanquished. And all my doubts satisfied, Heaven speed the undertaking!"[30]

Few black Philadelphians hearing or reading the dialogues packed their bags, left the city, and headed home to Africa. Rather they remonstrated in 1818 and 1819 against the Colonization Society and spoke with their feet when the ACS dispatched the first two ships to establish the colony of Liberia in 1819 and 1820. Of about 10,000 free black Philadelphians, only twenty-two joined the expedition, though economic conditions in the city had worsened greatly. A few years later, another recruitment campaign netted only another handful for settlement in Liberia.

By 1818, Tench Coxe must have wished that Philadelphia's black masses had opted for immigration to West Africa. The deep depression that followed the end of the War of 1812, the most severe ever experienced in the northern cities, may have shattered his earlier optimism about the assimilation of free black people and their potential as respectable citizens. Or had he fallen in line with the Jeffersonian faith in state-centered democracy, which was leading toward restrictions on black citizenship? Or had Philadelphia's white workingmen, who formed the Jeffersonian party's spine, changed his mind as they grew increasingly rabid on race issues? Or had the essays of men such as Charles Caldwell and Thomas Branagan reconfigured his thinking? Whatever the causes, Coxe reversed course, now viewing free African Americans concentrated in northern cities as an impoverished, uneducated mass for whom the rights of full citizenship were inappropriate.

But if free black people were a pariah group, how could their exclusion be squared with the avowed principles of color-blind citizenship that had prevailed for nearly half a century? Founding members of the American Colonization Society, which included some of the nation's most admired political leaders and thinkers, were constructing an answer. At ACS's first meeting, Henry Clay had argued that free black people were "a useless and pernicious, if not dangerous portion of [the nation's] population." Others knew that these gloomy characterizations promoted ideas about a fractured American identity. In following up on Clay's address, Elias Boudinot Caldwell, scion of a wealthy New Jersey family and Clerk of the Supreme Court, brooded about this. Quoting the founding fathers' axiom "that all men are created equal and have certain unalienable rights," Caldwell warned that the ACS was leading a cause ready to deny that *all* free Americans acquired citizenship by birthright. But Caldwell stumbled. Regrettably, he confessed, white hatred of black Americans made it impossible that "they can ever be placed upon this equality, or admitted to the enjoyment of these 'unalienable rights' while they remain mixed with us." "Some persons may declaim and call it prejudice," Caldwell admitted. But "no matter," he answered. "Prejudice is as powerful a motive, and will as certainly exclude them, as the soundest reason." Removing black Americans rather than removing white prejudice was winning the day. Caldwell was one of many leading white figures who chose to bow to popular feeling rather than seek to change it.[31]

The task of finding a rationale for denying citizenship to free black Americans without sacrificing principles to prejudice captured Tench Coxe's attention in 1820. Could he find a "theoretically consistent way to deny [free black people] the rights and privileges of citizens"?[32] This was precisely the question raised in Congress when the admission of the Missouri Territory to the union as a slave state, first broached in 1819, became a fiery, deeply divisive, and destabilizing issue. Slavery, the pro-southern argument went, had to be protected to preserve the nation's unity. In fact, however, a north-south unity purchased through the expansion of slavery into the western territories proved to be a tenuous unity, indeed a counterfeit recipe for union and a ticking time bomb of sectional tension.

By March 1820, after some of the most fiery debates in Congressional history, Congress decided it
did not have the power to forbid slavery in a state ap-
plying for entry into the Union. By admitting Maine
as a free state while Missouri entered the Union as
a slave state, Congress maintained sectional parity
in the Senate. Congress hoped to settle the issue by
drawing a line through the rest of the Louisiana Territory at 36 degrees, 30 minutes, a fateful marker for
defining slave and free territory for the future. But on
the heels of this compromise, a second issue arose—a
Missouri constitution passed in St. Louis in July 1820
that forbid the entry of free black Americans into the
new state. Many northern Congressmen strongly ob-
jected to this denial of a prime citizenship right of
free movement. Southerners vigorously defended the
offending clause, denying explicitly that free blacks
in the United States were citizens. This brought the
entire question about black citizenship to a head, in-
vesting it with "tremendous political and ideological
significance."[33]

If Congress supported the southern position that
free black people were not citizens (the position the
Supreme Court avowed forty years later in the *Dred
Scott* decision) then free black adults in the North, as
many northern Congressmen pointed out, would be

vulnerable to losing the right to move freely, acquire property, worship freely, and, correlatively, would be relieved of their obligation to pay taxes and defend their country. Pennsylvania's representative Joseph Hemphill put it bluntly: "If being a native, and free born, and of parents belonging to no other nation or tribe, does not constitute a citizen of this country, I am at a loss to know in which manner citizenship is acquired by birth." Senator Justin Morrill of New Hampshire argued that if Congress endorsed Missouri's constitution, making a distinction between citizens simply on the basis of color, then the precedent would be set for every state to grant or withhold rights similarly. In this case, "your national existence is lost; the Union is destroyed; the objects of confederation annihilated, and your political fabric is demolished." Secretary of State John Quincy Adams agreed that the Missouri constitutional clause would strip thousands of citizens of constitutionally guaranteed rights. "Already cursed by the mere color of their skin," he argued, "already doomed by their complexion to drudge in the lowest offices of society, excluded by their color from all the refined enjoyments of life accessible to others . . . this barbarous article deprives them of the little remnant of right yet left them—their rights as citizens and as men."[34]

Southerners responded, with withering facts at their disposal: every day of the week northern states discriminated against free black men and women and denied them full equality. Free black people were not in fact citizens—and were not treated so throughout much of the North. Especially, southerners argued, emancipated slaves were not free-born and were therefore incapable of acquiring citizenship simply because their masters relinquished claims to their labor.[35]

Into the midst of this heated argument over whether free black Americans were citizens, aliens, residents, or something else, Tench Coxe, writing at a blistering pace, submitted thirteen essays to the Philadelphia newspaper most popular among Jeffersonian workingmen and shopkeepers, the Negrophobic *Democratic Press*. He titled the essays "Considerations respecting the Helots of the United States, African and Indian, native and Alien, and their descendants of the whole and mixed blood." This was a tip-off since "helots" referred to a class of serfs in ancient Sparta who were neither slaves nor citizens—Coxe aimed to tilt Congress toward the southern view of black non-citizenship. Certainly his essays must have been greeted enthusiastically in the South, coming as they did from a "Philadelphia grandee" and a man who had served both as an important Federalist and Jeffersonian officeholder.[36]

At the heart of his essays, Coxe argued that free black Americans, Indians, and all people of mixed blood had never been considered a part of the social compact before the American Revolution and that in the Declaration of Independence and the state constitutions passed thereafter had never "been admitted to the rights of Citizenship." This blatantly disavowed what he had argued a few years before. Coxe did not relinquish the idea that slavery must end at some time in the future, and he was critical of northern states and municipalities for crippling the chances of free black people by denying them public education. But while hedging this hint that free black Americans were potentially worthy, he argued that the "Helots of America" were descended from "uncivilised or wild men without our moral sense . . . [or] our notions of moral character," a people "not yet evinced, by the actual facts, to be capable of genuine modern civilization." "Are we all willing to give them the whole substance of the liberty, wherewith heaven has made us free" he asked rhetorically; "or are the Helot people deemed unworthy to be made as consummately free citizens as ourselves; or are they considered incapable of attaining the characteristics, moral and intellectual, which belong to the least qualified portion of the white citizens in the states which admit to suffrage and office all but paupers and insane persons?"[37]

With this language, Coxe turned his back on the environmentalist beliefs subscribed by the Pennsylvania Abolition Society and aligned himself with the speculations about biological inferiority that Jefferson had spun out in his *Notes on Virginia* a quarter century before. Choosing the loaded word "helot," meaning serf or slave, to punctuate his essays, he joined the new pseudo-scientific school to revive the old view that black people of purported savage backgrounds could never overcome immutable traits that made them forever unsuitable for citizenship. "Are we ready to put the trials of the black and colored men into the hands of juries of their true and proper peers, full black and colored citizens, without limitation," Coxe asked. "Are we ready to put the defence of the characters of our sons and chaste honor of our wives & daughters, upon such panels, uninstructed as they come to us, from the slave estates?" Put this way, only one answer would serve: it was right, Coxe pronounced, that free black men were "excluded . . . from the rights, qualities, and character of citizens." Free black Americans would have to be removed to a "new Africa" somewhere in the remote West where they would be policed, reservation style, by the federal government.[38] Those still enslaved must remain so because injecting additional innately incapable men and women into southern communities as free people would bring on the "horror . . . of a *Helot convulsion*" and "the prostration of everything from the cradle of the infant to the couch of age, the bed of virgin purity, and the half sacred connubial chamber."[39] Coxe's biographer Jacob Cooke calls this a defense of slavery "that not even southern hard liners . . . could have bettered."[40]

Coxe's essays reflecting the growing white doctrine of innate black inferiority also contributed to undermining the belief that American nationality was based on laws and institutions, not skin color. He remained a nominal opponent of slavery, believing that "providence doubtless intends them [slaves]" for freedom. But he sternly lectured those who challenged slavery in the South, warning that this was reckless and would fatally wound the economic interests of the North that were becoming closely tied to the South's cotton-based slave economy.[41]

Why did Tench Coxe beat such a rapid retreat from his earlier position on free black entitlement to full citizenship? How came it, as his biographer puts it,

that "he had only to contemplate fleetingly the notion of [racial] equality to be thrown into frenzied
terror." By Coxe's own account, it was the wretched
condition of free African Americans in the North
that had "raised in the most favorable minds fears
that even gradual emancipation has lost much of its
supposed facility among men who consider the present and probable results of that interesting opera-
tion." Given the hapless condition of free black
northerners and the unwillingness of whites to edu-
cate them, he argued, black people must be "bound
to obey the exclusive legislative authority of the
white people."[42] Yet Coxe's change of attitude toward
black capability and entitlement to citizenship occurred during precisely the years when African American churches, schools, mutual aid associations, and
literary societies had built the foundations for a esti-
mable black citizenry while many black urban dwellers had carved out respectable niches in the economy.
Also indisputably, as Coxe had witnessed and wel-
comed along with all Philadelphians, the shovel brigades of black Philadelphians, along with Irish, German, and other men with roughened hands, had
marched out of town at the height of the War of 1812
to strengthen the fortifications protecting the city
against an attacking British navy. A careful auditor of

statistical information, Coxe also knew what the census of 1820 revealed—that among the city's two thousand black householders about one in eight was a property owner and many had achieved middle-class status. Many were his neighbors, men and women with whom he exchanged greetings on the streets from day to day.

Was it deliberate self-deception that led Coxe to argue that giving free black people full citizenship was misguided benevolence because it would "render the unfortunate black people objects of endless litigations, awful terrors, and fatal injuries?" The origins of Coxe's stunning turnabout are multiple. Certainly his change of heart partakes of the American Colonization Society's rise and its embrace by many white Philadelphians, including many of Coxe's friends and even some members of the Pennsylvania Abolition Society.[43] In a few short years since its founding in 1816, the ACS had crystallized the latent feeling—in white churches, in salon life, and in the counting houses of Philadelphia—that black people were not assimilable either because of innate black inferiority or because of obdurate white prejudice. Coxe's essays on "the American Helots" dovetailed neatly with the ACS's arguments, providing what historian Charles Sellers calls "a moral fig leaf to claim antislavery virtue without disturbing the economic/political status quo."[44]

Coxe's reversal of a deeply held commitment to racial equality also jibes with Rogers Smith's analysis of how northern industrial development altered ideas of citizenship. The slave-produced cotton from the South that set the spinning wheels of northern textile factories humming put a premium on men such as Coxe to change their views. Always a man with an eye toward political economy, Coxe was particularly attuned to how the wheels of industry, banking, and commerce turned in Pennsylvania. "To assuage their liberal consciences," writes Smith of northerners, "white Americans . . . began elaborating . . . defenses of their civic inequalities, buttressed by pseudo-scientific Enlightenment and Protestant religious doctrines of racial and cultural superiority. In so doing they tacked white supremacist qualifications onto a basically Lockean understanding of American political identity." When Thomas Morris, a Jacksonian senator from Ohio, thundered in 1839 that "the slave power of the South and the banking power of the North are now uniting to rule the country," he echoed the rhetorical stance newly adopted by Tench Coxe nearly twenty years before. In the early stages of the cotton revolution, which would soon

turn Philadelphia and other northern cities into textile processing centers, Coxe the herald of capitalist
development simultaneously became a herald of
white supremacy.[45]

Beyond the broader current of industrial change
that was carrying men like Coxe toward an alliance
with southern slaveholding interests, the controversy
over the Missouri Compromise provides a more specific context for his turnabout on black citizenship.
The Missouri agitation, wrote Elias Boudinot, the
grizzled New Jersey revolutionary leader now in his
eighties, "seems to have run alike a flaming fire thro
our middle states and causes great anxiety." Pennsylvania was of critical importance to proslavery southern Congressmen working for the admission of Missouri as a slave state, and Philadelphia was the center
of the manufacturers, bankers, and merchants with
close southern ties. Coxe plunged into the Missouri
controversy, after observing the founding of the Philadelphia antislavery newspaper *National Gazette* in
1819, the strident attack on slavery by its editor Robert Walsh, and the heightened antislavery rhetoric of
James Duane, editor of Philadelphia's *Aurora* in late
1820. Even more disturbing to Coxe was the unani-
mous resolution of Pennsylvania legislature late in
1819 urging the state's Congressmen in Washington

to vote against admitting Missouri to the Union if slavery was sanctioned there. "The whole will depend on Pennsylvania," wrote Jefferson to Albert Gallatin, Coxe's close friend, on December 26, 1820.[46]

By this time, Coxe was already composing his essays on "the Helots of America," which, as his biographer maintains, were precipitated by the Missouri controversy. Viewed as an extended counter-attack on Pennsylvanians and other northerners opposed to the extension of slavery to Missouri, they became an important cog in what New Jersey's Elias Boudinot believed was "a wheel within a wheel . . . some bargaining taking place between the East and Southern interests." Written in the pivotal state of Pennsylvania, Coxe's essays were meant to tilt Pennsylvanians and other northerners toward accepting the extension of slavery into Missouri and pacify proslavery southerners.[47]

No one can measure the exact effect of Coxe's essays on "The Helots of the United States." But surely they fed the tide of anti-black sentiment coursing through James Forten's Philadelphia and throughout the North.[48] One year after Coxe's essays appeared, New York's legislature imposed a race-specific property qualification that disenfranchised most free black men.[49] Within a few more years white marauders in Boston, New Haven, and Pittsburgh attacked the most tangible markers of free black accomplishment and respectability—African American churches and the homes of successful black urban dwellers. In 1829, whites attacked black churches and neighborhoods in Philadelphia and Cincinnati. Two years later, Philadelphia's leading Quaker reformer, Roberts Vaux, wrote discouragingly that "the policy, and power of the national and state government, are against [free black people]. The popular feeling is against them—the interests of our citizens are against them. The small degree of compassion once cherished toward them in the commonwealths which got rid of slavery, or which never were disfigured by it, appears to be exhausted. Their prospects either as free, or bond men, are dreary, and comfortless."[50] The way was paved for Pennsylvania's Constitutional Convention in 1837–38, which, as in most northern states, conferred universal white manhood suffrage for the first time while stripping black men of their vote. It was under this new definition of color-coded citizenship that thousands of black Pennsylvanians fought for the Union a quarter century later.

Though Coxe's essays fed the virulent proslavery, white supremacist campaign and contributed indirectly to southern slaveowning power in Congress, his literary productions became part of the pro-slavery stridency that spurred black organization, self-expression, and militancy. If it was not already clear before their publication, his essays showed free black Americans after 1820 that they faced a cruel double paradox. With the growing free black population demonstrating that slavery and blackness were no longer synonymous, white northerners "placed a premium on racial demarcation" to the disadvantage of blacks. At the same time, the more free black people achieved in building churches, schools, and mutual aid societies, the more white people resented them.[51] No black American in the North could escape this paradox. But resolving paradoxes is often the work of those who suffer its inequities and wounds. With civic-mindedness and moral rectitude, the earnests of good citizenship, no longer counting for much, black Americans had reached a watershed. Not given to despair and capitulation, they channeled anger, frustration, and disappointment into mobilization, where improvisation had to replace reliance on sweeping, clear-cut principles derived from the nation's founding documents. Before, the black preacher was—to use the words of W. E. B. Du Bois—"the most unique personality developed by the Negro on American soil." But after 1820, while black clergymen still stood as pillars of the black community, it was the secular leader, defiant rather than moderate, politically more than religiously attuned, who stepped toward center stage as a race-proud and uncompromising man. And as for black clergymen, they turned steadily from explanations of slavery and the slave trade as the mysterious workings of God's will to "free-will evangelicalism" that placed the blame for slavery squarely on ungodly human actors.[52]

Within a few years of Coxe's death in 1824, the first black newspaper in the United States, *Freedom's Journal*, launched a new era of black political consciousness and inter-city organization, all fueled by a growing stream of published sermons, speeches, and proceedings from inter-city black conventions. This showed that the Missouri Compromise, often said to take the question of slavery off the table for wearied Americans, did not quiet the controversy at all. Though white Americans reluctantly admitted it, or pretended it wasn't happening, a "river of struggle," as Vincent Harding has put it, "slowly, steadily developed its black power beneath the rough surfaces of the new nation." James Forten, now in his sixties, stands as an apt example. Becoming evermore active, as if to finish his life with a flourish that would coun-

teract the effects of his neighbor Tench Coxe's corrosive formulations about race and citizenship, he
penned an early contribution in 1827 to *Freedom's
Journal,* indicting Henry Clay's dishonesty in pretending to be the friend of oppressed black Americans
when his real intention, in promoting the American
Colonization Society, was to rid the South of free
black men and women whose presence threatened
slavery.[53] In 1829 Boston's David Walker published
the *Appeal to the Coloured Citizens of the World,* which
encouraged free black citizens to challenge white arguments such as those advanced by Coxe. Especially,
Walker nourished the belief, in prose that fairly
leaped off the page, that if America was truly to be a
redeemer nation, redemption of the nation's sins
would have to be the work of black, not white, Americans. Thus, in his "volume of fire," Walker called for
black Americans not only to "think and feel and act
as one solid body" but to see themselves as God's
chosen people, a people whose resistance to slavery
and white discrimination was divinely sanctioned.[54]

Two years later, as William Lloyd Garrison was preparing to launch his fiery abolitionist paper *The Liberator,* James Forten sent money for twenty-seven subscriptions that bought the ream of paper for the first
issue. In the first month of publication, Forten con

tributed another essay attacking colonization as a wicked scheme based on the noxious notion that "a [black] man is an alien to the country in which he was born." Forten carried on his struggle for another decade. When he died in 1841, he had given not an inch to his belief that "to separate the blacks from the whites is as impossible as to bail out the Delaware [River] with a bucket."[55]

Of course, white legislators *were* able to separate white and black Americans in civil and legal terms, at the cost of compromising the founding fathers' belief in birthright citizenship. But James Forten, black citizen and patriot of the revolutionary generation, passed the torch to a new generation of black leaders, who occupied the anomalous status of free *non*-citizens in a white man's country. They would have to cope with the northern support for proslavery southerners that Tench Coxe had helped to galvanize; and in Forten's Philadelphia they would have to gird their loins against the ever-strengthening nexus that linked the city's textile production with cotton-producing southern states. Yet whites, for all their power, whether in Philadelphia or elsewhere, could never sever free black Americans socially, economically, physically, or ideologically from American society at large. A people within a people perhaps, a nation within a nation, but nonetheless they were Americans. That this would remain overwhelmingly the commitment among African Americans was in no small part attributable to their remembrance and veneration of the black founding fathers and mothers of the revolutionary age, figures such as Richard Allen and James Forten of Philadelphia, Prince Hall and Phillis Wheatley of Boston, and similar touchstone figures whose names were invoked wherever free black people gathered in the young American nation.

NOTES

INDEX

# NOTES

### 1. The Black Americans' Revolution

1. The first pamphlet appeared in 1851 and the fuller
   version in 1855. Three years later, in 1858, Nell was
   among the Boston abolitionists who inaugurated
   Boston's Crispus Attucks Day. Thirty years later the
   Crispus Attucks monument rose in Boston, further
   thickening the black patriot myth. For Nell's career
   see Robert P. Smith, "William Cooper Nell: Cru-
   sading Black Abolitionist," *Journal of Negro History,*
   55 (1970), 182–199; and Dorothy Wesley Porter, "Inte-
   gration Versus Separatism: William Cooper Nell's
   Role in the Struggle for Equality," in Donald M.
   Jacobs, ed., *Courage and Conscience: Black and White
   Abolitionists in Boston* (Bloomington: Indiana University Press, 1993), 207–224.

2. See Nash, "Introduction" to reprint of Quarles, *The
   Negro in the American Revolution.* (Chapel Hill: University of North Carolina Press, 1996), xiii–xv. William Lloyd Garrison followed Nell's basic narrative

in 1860 when he published *The Loyalty and Devotion of Colored Americans in the Revolution and War of 1812.*

3. See Robert Benjamin Lewis, *Light and Truth* (1836), for the first book-length study of black history. Also see Hosea Easton, *Treatise on the Intellectual Character and Civil and Political Condition of the Colored People of the U.S.* (1837); and James W. C. Pennington, *A Text Book of the Origin and History of the Colored People* (Hartford: L. Skinner, 1841). Years ago the English historian J. H. Plumb spoke of the need to move away from "confirmatory history"—a "narration of events of *particular* people, nations or communities in order to justify authority, to create confidence and to secure stability" among powerholders. American historians have had no corner on "confirmatory history." As the Haitian historian-philosopher Michel-Rolph Trouillot tells us, it is nearly universal that history has been the province of the powerful, not the weak; the conquerors, not the conquered: "Lived inequalities," he writes, "yield unequal historical power."

4. Even W. E. B. Du Bois did not stray from the accepted formula of black revolutionary patriotism in the few references he made to the Revolution. See Herbert Aptheker's notes on Du Bois's columns in the *Pittsburgh Courier* for April 18, 1936, September 13, 1941, and April 24, 1948, where Du Bois spoke of black sacrifice in the American cause and the dis-

crimination black soldiers endured. Aptheker, *An Annotated Bibliography of the Writings of W. E. B. Du Bois* (Millwood, NY: Kraus-Thomson, 1973), 198, 388, 417, 466.

5. Fiske, *The American Revolution* (2 vols.; Boston: Houghton Mifflin, 1891), 1:178, quoted in Ray Raphael, *Founding Myths: Stories That Hide Our Patriotic Past* (New York: New Press, 2004), 181.

6. Aptheker, *The Negro in the American Revolution* (New York: International Publishers, 1940), 5–6.

7. For Lew see Sidney Kaplan and Emma Nogrady Kaplan, *The Black Presence in the Era of the American Revolution* (rev. ed.; Amherst: University of Massachusetts Press, 1989), 21–22; and Franklin A. Dorman, *Twenty Families of Color in Massachusetts, 1742–1998* (Boston: New England Historic Genealogical Society, 1998). The 5 percent calculation is figured by George Quintal Jr. in *Patriots of Color: "A Peculiar Beauty and Merit;" African Americans and Native Americans at Battle Road and Bunker Hill* (Boston: National Historical Park, 2002), 22.

8. Charles Patrick Neimeyer, *America Goes to War: A Social History of the Continental Army* (New York: New York University Press, 1996), 73. Of 4,400 free black people in Massachusetts during the war, not more than one-quarter could have been men of fighting age. The number of adult black males in the North could not have exceeded 10,000.

9.  Neimeyer, *America Goes to War,* 73. History buffs to-
    day can find Peter Salem portrayed by a National
    Park Service ranger at Minute Man National His-
    torical Park.

10. Legislature quoted in Fritz Hirschfeld, *George Wash-
    ington and Slavery: A Documentary Portrayal* (Colum-
    bia: University of Missouri Press, 1997), 148–149.
    Lorenzo Greene, "The Black Regiment of Rhode Is-
    land," *Journal of Negro History* 37 (1952), 144.

11. Peter Maslowski, "National Policy toward the Use
    of Black Troops in the Revolution," *South Carolina
    Historical Magazine* 73 (1972), 3–8; Gregory D.
    Massey, *John Laurens and the American Revolution*
    (Columbia: University of South Carolina Press,
    2000), 130–134. Many members of the Continental
    Congress would have known of the argument of
    the anonymous pamphleteer "Antibiastes," who ar-
    gued two years before that Congress should oversee
    a "general emancipation of the Slaves" who enlisted
    in the army and navy and provide proper compen-
    sation to their masters. "Antibiastes," *Observation on
    the Slaves and the Indented Servants, Inlisted in the
    Army, and in the Navy of the United States* (Philadel-
    phia, 1777).

12. Washington quoted in Henry Wiencek, *An Imperfect
    God: George Washington, His Slaves, and the Creation of
    America* (New York: Farrar, Straus and Giroux,

2003), 227. Gadsden quoted in Massey, *John Laurens,* 140.

13. Quoted in Bernard Bailyn, *The Ideological Origins of the American Revolution* (Cambridge, MA: Harvard University Press, 1967), 232–246. See also David Brion Davis, *The Problem of Slavery in Western Culture* (Ithaca: Cornell University Press, 1966), 441–442; and Duncan McLeod, *Slavery, Race, and the American Revolution* (Cambridge: Cambridge University Press, 1974), 14–31.

14. Arthur Lee, "Address on Slavery," *Virginia Gazette,* March 19, 1767, reprinted in Gary B. Nash, *Race and Revolution* (Madison, WI: Madison House, 1990), 92–96. Bailyn, *Ideological Origins,* 235.

15. Adams to Jeremy Belknap, March 21, 1795, Massachusetts Historical Society *Collections,* 5th ser., 3 (1877), 402.

16. Herbert Aptheker, *A Documentary History of the Negro People in the United States* (New York: Citadel, 1951), 2 vols., 1: 6–7.

17. Ibid., 7–8. The petitions are discussed in Thomas J. Davis, "Emancipation Rhetoric, Natural Rights, and Revolutionary New England: A Note on Four Black Petitions in Massachusetts, 1773–1777," *New England Quarterly,* 62 (1989), 248–263.

18. The petition is reprinted in part in Kaplan and Kaplan, *Black Presence,* 13, 15. Three years after

Boston slaves rebuked their masters for not affording them advantages given Spanish slaves under the custom of *coartación,* the British abolitionist Granville Sharp publicized these "Spanish Regulations" and urged British slave masters to follow them. Sharp, *The Just Limitations of Slavery . . . The Spanish Regulations for the gradual enfranchisement of Slaves . . .* (London, 1776), cited in Christopher Brown, "Envisioning an Empire without Slavery, 1772–1834," in Philip D. Morgan and Sean Hawkins, eds., *Black Experience and the Empire* (Oxford: Oxford University Press, 2004), 121.

19. For the role of the Quock Walker case in abolishing slavery judicially, see Arthur Zilversmit, "Quock Walker, Mumbet, and the Abolition of Slavery in Massachusetts," *William and Mary Quarterly,* 3d ser., 25 (1968), 614–624; and A. Leon Higginbotham Jr., *In the Matter of Color: Race and the American Legal Process, The Colonial Period* (New York: Oxford University Press, 1978), 91–98.

20. Mum Bett's story is well told in Kaplan and Kaplan, *Black Presence,* 244–248; Mum Bett's vow is in Catharine Maria Sedgwick, "Slavery in New England," *Bentley's Miscellany* (London, 1853), 34: 421; for Sedgwick's strong emotional ties to Mum Bett see Mary Kelley, ed., *The Power of Her Sympathy: The Autobiography and Journal of Catharine Maria Sedgwick*

(Boston: Massachusetts Historical Society, 1993), 15–17, 87, 124–126.

21. A small number of escaping slaves found refuge among Indian peoples west of the English settlements.

22. Abigail Adams to John Adams, September 22, 1774, in L. H. Butterfield et al., eds., *Adams Family Correspondence,* 6 vols. (Cambridge, Mass.: Harvard University Press, 1963–1993), 1: 161–162. Leonard Woods Labaree et al., eds., *The Papers of Benjamin Franklin,* 36 vols. (New Haven: Yale University Press, 1959–), 11: 397–399. Kaplan and Kaplan, *Black Presence,* 16.

23. Dunmore quoted in Woody Holton, *Forced Founders: Indians, Debtors, Slaves, and the Making of the Revolution in Virginia* (Chapel Hill: University of North Carolina Press, 1999), 141. The words from Dunmore's Proclamation that engulfed white southerners with fear while overjoying their chattel property read: "I do hereby . . . declare all indented servants, Negroes, or others (appertaining to Rebels) free, that are able and willing to bear arms, they joining His Majesty's Troops as soon as may be, for the more speedily reducing the Colony to a proper sense of their duty, to his Majesty's crown and dignity." For more on Dunmore's Proclamation as "the culmination of an existing trend rather than a dramatic departure," see Philip D. Morgan

and Andrew J. O'Shaughnessy, "Arming Slaves in the American Revolution," in Philip D. Morgan and Christopher L. Brown, eds., *Arming Slaves: From the Classical Era to the American Civil War* (New Haven: Yale University Press, forthcoming).

24. Lund Washington to George Washington, December 3, 1775, in Philander D. Chase et al., eds., *Papers of George Washington, Revolutionary War Series,* 12 vols. (Charlottesville: University Press of Virginia, 1988), 2: 480. For Williamsburg's remarkable revamping of historical memory, see Richard Handler and Eric Gable, *New History in an Old Museum: Creating the Past at Colonial Williamsburg* (Durham: Duke University Press, 1997); and Cary Carson, ed., *Becoming Americans: Our Struggle to Be Both Free and Equal* (Williamsburg: Colonial Williamsburg Foundation, 1998).

25. Holton, *Forced Founders,* 157; Cassandra Pybus, *Epic Journeys of Freedom: Runaway Slaves of the American Revolution and Their Global Quest for Liberty* (Boston: Beacon Press, 2005), ch. 3. One of those who fled, a woman in her late thirties, became part of the exodus of former slaves who returned to Sierra Leone twenty years later. There she related how she was converted to Methodism while still a slave in Virginia and would walk ten miles at night with her small daughter strapped to her back to join other black worshipers seeking solace in evangelical Christianity.

26. Dunmore believed that about two thousand slaves had reached his lines; Dunmore to Secretary of State Lord George Germain, June 26, 1776, in William Bell Clark, ed., *Naval Documents of the American Revolution,* 10 vols. (Washington: Government Printing Office, 1964–96), 5: 756. Jefferson to John Randolph, November 29, 1775, in Julian P. Boyd, ed., *The Papers of Thomas Jefferson,* 31 vols. (Princeton: Princeton University Press, 1960–), 1: 268–270.

27. William Byrd III killed himself on New Year's Eve, 1776, deeply in debt to British merchants and perhaps disconsolate at his son's defection to the British. See Holton, *Forced Founders,* 156, and John E. Selby, *The Revolution in Virginia, 1775–1783* (Charlottesville: University Press of Virginia, 1988), 67.

28. Quarles, *Negro in the American Revolution,* 30; Elizabeth Fenn, *Pox Americana: The Great Smallpox Epidemic of 1775–82* (New York: Hill and Wang, 2001), 58–61.

29. *The Journals of Henry Melchior Muhlenberg,* trans. Theodore G. Tappert and Johan W. Doberstein, 3 vols. (Philadelphia: German Society of Pennsylvania, 1942–58), 3: 78; *Pennsylvania Packet,* January 1, 1780. For a fuller account of the slave flight to the British in the Philadelphia region, see Nash, *Forging Freedom,* 45–46.

30. William Moultrie, *Memoirs of the American Revolution,* 2 vols. (New York: David Longworth, 1802), 1:

259, quoted in Sylvia R. Frey, *Water from the Rock: Black Resistance in a Revolutionary Age* (Princeton: Princeton University Press, 1991), 85.

31. Quotations from Frey, *Water from the Rock,* 152, 156–157, 159. In the flight of slaves during the British southern campaigns of 1780–1782, I have focused only on Virginia, leaving aside the cases of Georgia and the Carolinas. Frey (chs. 3–4) covers the massive slave defections to the British. The defection rate was probably even higher than in Virginia, partly because British forces were there for more prolonged periods and also because intense internecine warfare between loyalist and patriot slaveowners gave slaves unusual chances to escape. An argument for scaling back the number of black defectors is made by Cassandra Pybus in "Jefferson's Faulty Math: The Question of Slave Defections in the American Revolution," *William and Mary Quarterly,* 57 (2005), 243–264.

32. Lucia Stanton, *Free Some Day: The African-American Families of Monticello* (Charlottesville: Thomas Jefferson Foundation, 2000), 56–57; Jefferson's list of slaves who fled to the British, recorded in his farm book, is reproduced on p. 52. Fenn, *Pox Americana,* 129. Frey, *Water from the Rock,* 167–168, quoting from James Curtis Ballagh, ed., *The Letters of Richard Henry Lee,* 2 vols. (New York: Macmillan, 1914), 2: 242, 256. Johann von Ewald, *Diary of the American*

*War: A Hessian Journal,* trans. and ed. Joseph P. Tustin (New Haven: Yale University Press, 1979), 305.

33.  Honyman and Lee quoted in Frey, *Water from the Rock,* 168. The majority stayed where they were; but we need to appreciate that a great many of these stay-at-homes were children too young to make any kind of move, pregnant or suckling women with limited chances of surviving a flight to the British, disabled and elderly slaves with limited physical capabilities, and an abundance of others who prized the place where they lived and feared the uncertainty of life with the rarely reliable British.

34.  Ewald, *Diary of the American War,* 305.

35.  Josiah Atkins Diary, quoted in Fenn, *Pox Americana,* 129.

36.  Ewald, *Diary of the American War,* 335–336. Private Joseph Plumb Martin also saw "herds of Negroes" in the woods, "scattered about in every direction, dead and dying with pieces of ears of burnt Indian corn in the hands and mouths, even of those that were dead." James Kirby Martin, ed., *Ordinary Courage: The Revolutionary War Adventures of Joseph Plumb Martin* (1830; St. James, NY: Brandywine Press, 1993), 141–142.

37.  O'Hara quoted in Fenn, *Pox Americana,* 130.

38.  Martin, *Ordinary Courage,* 141–142.

39.  Pybus, *Epic Journeys,* ch. 3.

40.  Stanton, *Free Some Day,* 52–57.

41. Frey, *Water from the Rock*, 174.

42. Planter quoted in Robert Olwell, *Masters, Slaves, and Subjects: The Culture of Power in the South Carolina Low Country, 1740–1790* (Ithaca: Cornell University Press, 1998), 269. Rutledge quoted in Frey, *Water from the Rock*, 178.

43. Olwell, *Masters, Slaves, and Subjects*, 269.

44. Frey, *Water from the Rock*, 177. These numbers make the estimate of 25,000 South Carolina slaves fleeing the British, made after the war by David Ramsay, doctor and historian of the Revolution in South Carolina, seem reasonable. Working from the estimates of "good judges," he believed slaveowners lost more than one-quarter of their 90,000 slaves. *Ramsay's History of South Carolina from Its First Settlement in 1670 to the Year 1808* (Newberry, SC: W. J. Duffie, 1858), 2 vols., 2: 271–272. Pybus estimates that 7,000 to 8,000 blacks were evacuated from Charleston. *Jubilee Is Come*, ch. 4.

45. George Smith McCowen, *The British Occupation of Charleston, 1780–82* (Columbia: South Carolina University Press, 1972), 149n.

46. Frey, *Water from the Rock*, 180–183.

47. *Memoirs of the Life of Boston King, a Black Preacher* [London, 1798], in Vincent Carretta, ed., *Unchained Voices: An Anthology of Black Authors in the English-Speaking World of the Eighteenth Century* (Lexington: University of Kentucky Press, 1996), 356.

48. Ibid. The pilgrimage to Nova Scotia is told fully in Ellen Gibson Wilson, *The Loyal Blacks* (New York: Putnam, 1976); James W. St. G. Walker, *The Black Loyalists: The Search for a Promised Land in Nova Scotia and Sierra Leone, 1783–1870* (New York: Africana Publishing, 1976); and Tybus, *Epic Journeys,* ch. 4.

49. Stephen Braidwood, *Black Poor and White Philanthropists: London's Blacks and the Foundations of the Sierra Leone Settlement, 1786–1791* (Liverpool, 1994).

50. Cassandra Pybus, "Black Refugees of the American Revolution," manuscript, 15. Ralph Henry, former slave of Patrick Henry; Harry Washington, former slave of George Washington; and several former slaves of John Jay are among the names in the Book of Negroes. The ship carrying Thomas Peters, a slave from Wilmington, North Carolina, along with his wife and two children, blew off course, and they sought refuge in Bermuda for the winter of 1783. They set forth the following spring, reaching Nova Scotia in May, months after the rest of the black settlers had arrived. Peters led his family ashore at Annapolis Royal, a small port on the east side of the Bay of Fundy that looked across the water to the coast of Maine. There he became a leader of the African Canadians for nearly a decade. Then, like a Black Moses, he led them back across the Atlantic in 1792 to a new promised land in Sierra Leone. See Nash, "Thomas Peters: Millwright and Deliverer,"

in David G. Sweet and Gary B. Nash, eds., *Struggle and Survival in Colonial America* (Berkeley: University of California Press, 1981), 76–84.

51. Bernard Bailyn, *To Begin the World Anew: The Genius and Ambiguities of the Founding Fathers* (New York: Knopf, 2003), 5, 35–36.

52. Lewis V. Baldwin, *Invisible Strands in African Methodism: A History of the African Union Methodist Protestant and Union African Methodist Episcopal Churches, 1805–1980* (Philadelphia: American Theological Library Association, 1983), 24. Thomas Coke, an early white Methodist leader, called Hosier "one of the best preachers in the world." Ibid.

53. William J. Wilson, quoted in Patrick Rael, *Black Identity and Black Protest in the Antebellum Era* (Chapel Hill: University of North Carolina Press, 2002), 1.

54. Richard Allen's manumission papers, copied into the Manumission Books of the Pennsylvania Abolition Society, at the Historical Society of Pennsylvania, show that he was to pay sixty pounds gold and silver, or two thousand Continental dollars, to his master in five yearly installments. He paid the freedom price in about eighteen months. See Nash, "New Light on Richard Allen: The Early Years," *William and Mary Quarterly,* 3d ser., 46 (1989), 332–340.

55. W. E. B. Du Bois, *The Philadelphia Negro: A Social*

*Study* (1899; New York: Schocken, 1967), 21. Albert Raboteau calls the AME "arguably the most important African-American institution for most of the nineteenth century" in *A Fire in the Bones: Reflections on African-American Religious History* (Boston: Beacon Press, 1995), 79. For the emergence of "vigorous literary production" among free blacks in the post-revolutionary period see Joanna Brooks, "The Early American Public Sphere and the Emergence of a Black Print Counterpublic," *William and Mary Quarterly,* 3d ser., 62 (2005), 67–92.

56. John Saillant, *Black Puritan, Black Republican: The Life and Thought of Lemuel Haynes, 1753–1833* (New York: Oxford University Press, 2003), 47, 49.

57. Kaplan and Kaplan, *Black Presence,* 120.

58. Evelyn Gerson, "Ona Judge Staines: Escape from Washington," www.seacoastnh.com/blackhistory/ona.html. Two articles from New Hampshire newspapers in the 1840s on Staines's life can be read at www.ushistory.org/presidentshouse/slaves.

59. Gerson, "Ona Judge Staines."

60. The accolade is from George Washington Parke Custis, Martha Washington's grandson. Custis's extended description of Hercules is in Custis, *Recollections and Private Memoirs of the Life and Character of Washington,* ed. Benson J. Lossing (New York, 1860), 422–424. For more on Hercules, see Henry Wiencek,

*An Imperfect God: George Washington, His Slaves, and the Creation of America* (New York: Farrar, Straus and Giroux, 2003), 314–320.

61. Washington to Tobias Lear, April 12, 1791, quoted in Wiencek, *Imperfect God,* 315–316; Louis-Philippe, King of France, *Diary of My Travels in America,* trans. Stephen Becker (New York: Delacorte Press, 1977), 31.

62. For the comment of Hercules' daughter, see www.ushistory.org/presidentshouse/slaves/hercules.htm.

63. Washington Curtis, her grandson, wrote that "it was found necessary (for prudential reasons) to give them their freedom in one year after the general's decease." Quoted in Wiencek, *Imperfect God,* 358.

## 2. Could Slavery Have Been Abolished?

1. In "The Central Themes of the American Revolution: An Interpretation," Bernard Bailyn approves of "their refusal . . . to allow the Revolutionary movement to slide off into fanaticism" and deems Jefferson "the supreme exemplar" of the "practical and moderate" men who led the Revolution and could not be expected "to transcend altogether the limitations of their own age." In Stephen Kurtz, ed., *Essays on the American Revolution* (Chapel Hill: University of North Carolina Press, 1973), 28–29. By the

1830s, after the advent of radical abolitionism, "fanatical" became a stock word, along with "distempered" and "enthusiastical," in the glossary of proslavery writers, though Larry Tise has found a rare use of it as early as 1773; see Tise, *Proslavery: A History of the Defense of Slavery in America, 1701–1840* (Athens: University of Georgia Press, 1987), 29.

2. David Brion Davis, *The Problem of Slavery in the Age of Revolution, 1770–1823* (Ithaca: Cornell University Press, 1975). David Waldstreicher, *Runaway America: Benjamin Franklin, Slavery, and the American Revolution* (New York: Hill and Wang, 2004), 232. Other important studies of abolitionism in the revolutionary age include Arthur Zilversmit, *The First Emancipation: The Abolition of Slavery in the North* (Chicago: University of Chicago Press, 1967); Betty Fladeland, *Men and Brothers: Anglo-American Antislavery Cooperation* (Urbana: University of Illinois Press, 1972); Joanne Pope Melish, *Disowning Slavery: Gradual Emancipation and "Race" in New England, 1780–1860* (Ithaca: Cornell University Press, 1998); and Richard S. Newman, *The Transformation of American Abolitionism: Fighting Slavery in the Early Republic* (Chapel Hill: University of North Carolina Press, 2002).

3. Isaiah Berlin, *Historical Inevitability* (1955), quoted in Gary B. Nash, "The Concept of Inevitability in the History of European-Indian Relations," in Carla

Gardina Pestana and Sharon V. Salinger, eds., *Inequality in Early America* (Hanover: University Press of New England, 1999), 270–273. Berlin was not writing about the specific problem I address here, but his essay on historical inevitability fits the case: "Acts hitherto regarded as wicked or unjustifiable are seen in a more 'objective' fashion—in the larger context—as part of the process of history which, being responsible for providing us with our scale of values, must not therefore be judged in terms of it."

4. Jefferson quoted in Gary B. Nash, *Race and Revolution* (Madison, WI: Madison House, 1988), 16. The mid-nineteenth-century historian Richard Hildreth agreed that "the abolition of slavery was desired for their own states by all the more intelligent citizens of Maryland and Virginia, even more ardently than anywhere at the North." Hildreth, *Despotism in America: An Inquiry into the Nature, Results, and Legal Basis of the Slave-Holding System* (Boston: John P. Jewett, 1854), 302.

5. Don E. Fehrenbacher, *The Slaveholding Republic: An Account of the United States Government's Relations to Slavery* (New York: Oxford University Press, 2001), 254, 259. Tise, *Proslavery*, 29–35. Tise argues that "southern leaders, in their contacts with the outside world and their private correspondence, generally condemned slavery as an evil that could be removed as soon as possible" (35).

6. Melish, *Disowning Slavery,* 57–62. "Some Thoughts
   on the Subject of Freeing the Negro Slaves in the
   Colony of Connecticut" by Levi Hart, a respected
   New Divinity clergyman, was endorsed by Rhode Island's influential minister Samuel Hopkins. Care-
   fully calculating the number and age of slaves in
   Connecticut and fair compensation to owners for
   the remaining years of their slaves' labor, Hart reckoned that a one-time tax of three pence per pound
   of assessable property (a 1.25 percent increase in
   taxation for one year) would secure the freedom of
   all Connecticut slaves.

7. Peter Onuf, *Statehood and Union: A History of the
   Northwest Ordinance* (Bloomington: Indiana University Press, 1987), 42–45. Pelatiah Webster's *Essay on
   the Extent and Value of our Western Unlocated Lands*
   (1781) spread the knowledge of half a billion acres
   available to the nation's government. By 1790,
   about 70,000 acres had been sold in the Kentucky
   district, a mere drop compared to the 1.5. million
   acres sold to the Ohio Company for a bargain
   $500,000.

8. Freneau quoted in James Alexander Dun, "Dangerous Intelligence: Slavery, Race, and St. Domingue
   in the Early American Republic" (Ph.D. diss.,
   Princeton University, 2004), 196, citing *National Gazette,* January 5, 1792.

9. The first of these works was Maurice Morgann's *A

*Plan for the Abolition of Slavery in the West Indies* (London, 1772). See Christopher L. Brown, "Envisioning an Empire without Slavery, 1772–1834," in Philip D. Morgan and Sean Hawkins, eds., *Black Experience and the Empire* (Oxford: Oxford University Press, 2004), 114–127; and Steven Mintz, "Models of Emancipation during the Age of Revolution," *Slavery and Abolition* 17 (1996), 1–21.

10. Martin quoted in Davis, *Problem of Slavery,* 323. Also in 1788, William Pinkney, speaking in the Maryland legislature, struck a similar position. See Henry Wheaton, *Some Account of the Life, Writings, and Speeches of William Pinkney* (Philadelphia: Carey & Lea, 1826), 8–19.

11. John Bernard, *Retrospections of America, 1797–1811* (New York: Harper and Brothers, 1877), 90–91 in 1989 ed., quoted in Fritz Hirschfield, *Washington and Slavery* (Columbia: University of Missouri Press, 1997), 73.

12. Madison quoted in Donald Robinson, *Slavery in the Structure of American Politics, 1765–1820* (New York: Norton, 1979), 188, and in Drew R. McCoy, *The Last of the Fathers: James Madison and the Republican Legacy* (Cambridge: Cambridge University Press, 1989), 261–262.

13. Lynch and Rutledge quoted in Robinson, *Slavery in the Structure of American Politics,* 223.

14. Edward J. Cashin, "'But Brothers, It Is Our Land We

Are Talking About': Winners and Losers in the
Georgia Backcountry," in Ronald Hoffman, Thad
W. Tate, and Peter J. Albert, eds., *An Uncivil War: The
Southern Backcountry during the American Revolution*
(Charlottesville: University Press of Virginia, 1985),
245. Embroiled in an Indian war, Georgians had
contributed little to the revolutionary effort, ap-
pealing forlornly for help from the Continental
Congress.

15. Moultrie quoted in Robert M. Weir, "'The Violent
Spirit,' the Reestablishment of Order, and the Con-
tinuity of Leadership in Post-Revolutionary South
Carolina," in Hoffman, Tate, and Albert, eds., *Uncivil War,* 76. James Haw, *John and Edward Rutledge of
South Carolina* (Athens: University of Georgia Press,
1997), 175. R. Don Higginbotham, *The War of American Independence: Military Attitudes, Policies, and Practice, 1763–1789* (New York: Macmillan, 1971), 361, 375.

16. Randolph C. Downes, "Creek-American Relations,
1782–1790," *Georgia Historical Quarterly* 21 (1937), 162–
163; Arthur Preston Whitaker, "Alexander
McGillivray, 1783–1789," *North Carolina Historical Review* 5 (1928), 198. Michael D. Green, "Alexander
McGillivray," in R. David Edmunds, *American Indian Leaders: Studies in Diversity* (Lincoln: University
of Nebraska Press, 1980), 53.

17. *Annals of Congress,* 1 Cong., 1 Sess., 696–703.

18. Cathy D. Matson and Peter S. Onuf, *A Union of In-*

*terests: Political and Economic Thought in Revolutionary America* (Lawrence: University Press of Kansas, 1990). Rutledge quoted in Haw, *John and Edward Rutledge,* 198.

19. James Monroe to Patrick Henry, August 12, 1786, quoted in Staughton Lynd, *Class Conflict, Slavery, and the United States Constitution* (Indianapolis: Bobbs Merrill, 1967), 171.

20. Jefferson to Richard Price, August 7, 1785, in Julian Boyd, ed., *The Papers of Thomas Jefferson* (Princeton: Princeton University Press, 1950–), 31 vols., 8:356. Madison to Robert J. Evans, June 15, 1819, in *Letters and Other Writings of James Madison* (Philadelphia: J. B. Lippincott, 1865), 4 vols., 3: 135.

21. Matson and Onuf, *A Union of Interests,* 115–123.

22. The Quaker and PAS petitions are in *Annals of Congress,* 1 Cong., 2 Sess., 1182–84 and 1197–98; the committee report is in Linda Grant DePauw et al., eds., *Documentary History of the First Federal Congress of the United States of America* (Baltimore: Johns Hopkins University Press, 1972–2004), 17 vols., 3: 340–341. The fullest analysis of the debate is Howard A. Ohline, "Slavery, Economics, and Congressional Politics, 1790," *Journal of Southern History* 46 (1980), 335–360.

23. Philadelphia *General Advertiser,* 2 October 1792, quoted in Dun, "Dangerous Intelligence," 245. Roger Kennedy, *Mr. Jefferson's Lost Cause: Land, Farmers, Slavery, and the Louisiana Purchase* (New

York: Oxford University Press, 2003), 77; Stephen
Aron, *How the West Was Lost: The Transformation of
Kentucky from Daniel Boone to Henry Clay* (Baltimore:
Johns Hopkins University Press, 1996), 89–95.

24. Fairfax, "Plan for Liberating the Negroes within the
United States," *American Museum* 8 (December
1790), 285–287; Baltimore proposal in Philadelphia
*General Advertizer*, 18 October 1790. In late 1794 Phil-
adelphia's Benjamin Rush offered the Pennsylvania
Abolition Society 5,200 acres of land in western
Pennsylvania for the settlement of freed slaves from
southern states. Rush to President of PAS, in L. H.
Butterfield, ed., *Letters of Benjamin Rush* (Princeton:
Princeton University Press, 1951), 2 vols., 2:754–756.

25. Among many examples are John Calhoun's opposition to the Mexican-American War when his section of the country rabidly supported it, and Stephen Douglas's willingness to oppose his president,
his party, and his section of the country in fighting
the admission of Kansas as the fifteenth slave state
under the Lecompton Constitution.

26. Joyce Appleby, *Thomas Jefferson* (New York: Times
Books, 2003), 139. Allan Nevins's words, in his foreword to John F. Kennedy's *Profiles in Courage* (New
York: Harper Brothers, 1955), xix–xx, ring true: "It is
to the President that the nation looks for the type
of courage that places the whole national interest
above section, party, social group, or economic

193

bloc." It is "the qualities of Mr. Standfast and Valiant-for-Truth in the battle against Apollyon" that constitute political courage.

27. Merrill Jensen, ed., *The Documentary History of the Ratification of the Constitution,* vol. 2 of *Ratification of the Constitution by the States* (Madison: State Historical Society of Wisconsin, 1976), 417, 499. Wilson's remarks were made in response to complaints of Pennsylvanians that the Constitution left slavery intact.

28. Waldstreicher, *Runaway America,* 238–39. When Franklin died three weeks after "Sidi Mehemet Ibrahim on the Slave Trade" appeared in the *Federal Gazette,* Bob, the slave Franklin had "loaned" to his son-in-law, found he was a free man by the provisions of his owner's will.

29. David McCullough, *John Adams* (New York: Simon and Schuster, 2001), 133. Robinson, *Slavery in the Structure of American Politics,* 26–27. Patricia Bradley, in *Slavery, Propaganda and the American Revolution* (Jackson: University Press of Mississippi, 1998), shows that Adams's soft-pedaling on the issue of slavery had its origins much earlier. In the early 1770s, he "was building an intercolonial movement that avoided direct confrontation on the issue of slavery" (64, 80).

30. Adams to Jeremy Belknap, March 21, 1795, and Oc-

tober 22, 1795, in *Collections of the Massachusetts Historical Society,* 5th ser., III (Boston, 1877), 401, 416.

31. For the unwillingness of Massachusetts merchants and politicians to support abolition on the grounds that it would injure their efforts "to court southern concessions to northern economic plans" see Newman, *Transformation of American Abolitionism,* 35–37. It says volumes that in the most authoritative study of the gradual extinction of slavery in New England, from 1780 to 1860, the name John Adams never appears. Melish, *Disowning Slavery.*

32. Rogers M. Smith, *Civic Ideals: Conflicting Visions of Citizenship in U.S. History* (New Haven: Yale University Press, 1997), 138–139. John P. Kaminski, *A Necessary Evil? Slavery and the Debate over the Constitution* (Madison, WI: Madison House, 1995), 143.

33. John T. Noonan Jr., *Persons and Masks of the Law: Cardozo, Holmes, Jefferson, and Wythe as Makers of the Mask* (New York: Farrar, Straus and Giroux, 1976), 29. Jefferson to Price, 7 August 1785, in *Papers of Jefferson,* 8:356–357; for Jefferson's view that "a purer character has never lived" than Wythe and other such encomiums, see Julian P. Boyd and W. Edwin Hemphill, *The Murder of George Wythe: Two Essays* (Williamsburg: Institute of Early American History and Culture, 1955), 5–7.

34. Alonzo Thomas Dill, *George Wythe: Teacher of Liberty*

(Williamsburg: Independence Bicentennial Commission, 1979), 52–53. Robert B. Kirtland, *George Wythe: Lawyer, Revolutionary, Judge* (New York: Garland, 1986), 149 (quotation).

35. Philip Hamilton, *The Making and Unmaking of a Revolutionary Family: The Tuckers of Virginia, 1752–1830* (Charlottesville, University Press of Virginia, 2003), 63, 78–80.

36. Charles Cullen, *St. George Tucker and Law in Virginia* (New York: Garland, 1989), 120, 149–150, 189.

37. Henry Wiencek, *An Imperfect God: George Washington, His Slaves, and the Creation of America* (New York: Farrar, Straus and Giroux, 2003), 251. Lafayette had lost his own father when he was a teenager. From the time Washington sent the nineteen-year-old Lafayette into battle at Brandywine in September 1777, they became surrogate father and son. Calling Washington "my adoptive father," Lafayette named his first son George Washington Lafayette. Ibid., 261.

38. Lafayette to Washington, February 5, 1783, in Stanley J. Idzerda, ed., *Lafayette in the Age of the American Revolution: Selected Letters and Papers* (Ithaca: Cornell University Press, 1977–1983), 5 vols., 5: 90–93.

39. Washington and Gordon quoted in Wiencek, *Imperfect God,* 262. Gordon to Washington, August 30, 1784, *The Papers of George Washington, Confederation Series,* II, ed. W. W. Abbot and Dorothy Twohig

(Charlottesville: University Press of Virginia, 1992), 64.

40. Albert Matthews, "Notes on the Proposed Abolition of Slavery in Virginia in 1785," Colonial Society of Massachusetts *Publications,* 6 (1904), 376–377. Paul Finkelman, *Slavery and the Founders: Race and Liberty in the Age of Jefferson* (Armonk, NY: W. E. Sharpe, 1996), 106. Madison to Washington, November 11, 1785, in *The Papers of James Madison,* ed. William T. Hutchinson and William M. E. Rachel (Chicago: Chicago University Press, 1962–), 8: 403.

41. Harriet Martineau, "Views of Slavery and Emancipation," *Society in America* (New York: Saunders and Otley, 1837), 22. Paul Finkelman, *The Law of Freedom and Bondage: A Casebook* (New York: Oceana Publications, 1986), 116.

42. Pleasants to Washington, December 11, 1785, in Roger Bruns, ed., *Am I Not a Man and a Brother? The Antislavery Crusade of Revolutionary America, 1688–1788* (New York: Chelsea House, 1977), 508–509.

43. Quotations from Wiencek, *Imperfect God,* 261, 263.

44. Ibid., 273, 274–277.

45. Carter quoted in Andrew Levy, *The First Emancipator: The Radical Life of Robert Carter III, America's Forgotten Revolutionary* (New York: Random House, 2005), 231. On Carter's land and slaveholding, see Louis Morton, *Robert Carter of Nomini Hall: A Virginia Tobacco Planter of the Eighteenth Century* (Char-

lottesville: University Press of Virginia, 1941), 279–
290. For the influence of Methodists in convincing
many to divest themselves of slaves, see Dee E. An-
drews, *The Methodists and Revolutionary America,
1760–1800: The Shaping of an Evangelical Culture*
(Princeton: Princeton University Press, 2000), 124–
132.

46. The will is reprinted in Melvin Patrick Levy, *Israel
on the Appomattox: A Southern Experiment in Black
Freedom from the 1790s through the Civil War* (New
York: Knopf, 2004), 447–449.

47. Hamilton, *Making and Unmaking of a Revolutionary
Family*, 82–83.

48. Dumas Malone, *Thomas Jefferson as Political Leader*
(Berkeley: University of California Press, 1963), 10.
Bernard Bailyn, *To Begin the World Anew: The Genius
and Ambiguities of the American Founders* (New York:
Knopf, 2003), 42. In explaining Jefferson's "strange
reversal" on slavery—his support for its expansion
into Missouri and other parts of the New South
and his refusal as president to help Haiti after the
slaves there overthrew the vicious French regime—
Bailyn at first cites Jefferson's belief that "freeing
the slaves would imperil the survival of the [white]
nation's freedom" (48). How this might be so is left
unexplained. But Bailyn's larger argument is that
Jefferson abandoned abolitionist inclinations out
of fear of the growing "northern economic power"

that he believed would corrupt his concept of a white yeoman's republic (49–52). For Jefferson's abandonment of revolutionary principles in the face of black rebellion in Haiti, see Michael Zuckerman, "The Power of Blackness: Thomas Jefferson and the Revolution in St. Domingue," in Zuckerman, *Almost Chosen People: Oblique Biographies in the American Grain* (Berkeley: University of California Press, 1993), 175–218.

49. Zuckerman, "Power of Blackness," 201. Garrison quoted in David Brion Davis, *Was Thomas Jefferson an Authentic Enemy of Slavery?* (Oxford: Clarendon Press, 1970), 4.

50. Created as a memorial to the 250th anniversary of his birth, *The Worlds of Thomas Jefferson at Monticello* (New York: Thomas Jefferson Memorial Foundation, 1993) celebrates Jefferson the polymath and Jefferson the aesthete; but the display of Jefferson's lavish furnishings at Monticello is a spectacular testimony to choices he made between material possessions and human property.

51. Kosciuszko's will "authorize[d] my friend Thomas Jefferson to employ the whole [estate] thereof in purchasing Negroes from among his own or any others and giving them Liberty in my name." See Edward P. Alexander, "Jefferson and Kosciuszko: Friends of Liberty and of Man," *Pennsylvania Magazine of History and Biography* 92 (1968), 87–103; and

Louis Ottenberg, "A Testamentary Tragedy: Jefferson and the Wills of General Kosciuszko," *American Bar Association Journal* 44 (1958), 22–26. For Jefferson's estimate of the average value of slaves, see his letter to Jared Sparks, February 4, 1824, in *The Works of Thomas Jefferson,* ed. Paul Leicester Ford, 12 vols. (New York: Putnam, 1904–1905), 12:335–336.

52. Malone, *Jefferson as Political Leader,* 3. Robert F. Berkhofer Jr., "Jefferson, the Ordinance of 1784, and the Origins of the American Territorial System," *William and Mary Quarterly,* 3d ser., 29 (1972), 231–262.

53. Kennedy, *Jefferson's Lost Cause,* 29. Appleby, *Thomas Jefferson,* 136. Appleby, a leading Jefferson scholar, regards Jefferson's "greatest gift" as that of "inspiring others with his rhetoric." Ibid., 135. Davis, *Was Jefferson an Authentic Enemy of Slavery,* 11. Davis argues that Jefferson's "icy caution provided a precedent and model for the younger generation of politicians from both North and South who would attack every effort to discuss the slavery question as a reckless tampering with the 'seals' which Jefferson and the other Founders had 'wisely placed' on the nation's most incendiary issue." Ibid.

54. Fehrenbacher, *Slaveholding Republic,* 259–260.

55. Fehrenbacher writes: "It seems incredible that no one made an attempt to exclude slavery from the

northern part of the Louisiana Purchase as an off-
set to allowing it in the southern part." Ibid., 261.
Robert McColley notes that Jefferson "has been recognized universally as the father of exclusion [of
slavery] in the Old Northwest, but has never been
labeled the father of slavery in Louisiana except by
a few seething Federalists in his own day."
McColley, *Slavery and Jeffersonian Virginia,* 2nd ed.
(Champaign: University of Illinois Press, 1973), 125.

56. *Works of Jefferson,* 1: 77. "Thomas Jefferson," notes
Winthrop Jordan, "wrote more extensively and
more negatively than any other of his important
contemporaries about the natural mental capacities of 'negroes.'" Jordan, "Hemings and Jefferson:
Redux," in Jan Ellen Lews and Peter Onuf, eds.,
*Sally Hemings and Thomas Jefferson: History, Memory,
and Civic Culture* (Charlottesville: University Press of
Virginia, 1993), 37.

57. David Grimsted, "Anglo-American Racism and
Phillis Wheatley's 'Sable Veil,' 'Length'ned Chain,'
and 'Knitted Heart,'" in Ronald Hoffman and Peter
J. Albert, eds., *Women in the Age of the American Revolution* (Charlottesville: University Press of Virginia,
1989), 415. John Chester Miller, *Wolf by the Ears:
Thomas Jefferson and Slavery* (New York: Free Press,
1977), 96–97.

58. Grimsted, "Anglo-American Racism," 345, 431.

59. Quoted in Winthrop D. Jordan, *White over Black: American Attitudes toward the Negro, 1550–1812* (Chapel Hill: University of North Carolina Press, 1968), 454.

60. Grimsted, "Anglo-American Racism," 414–415.

61. Banneker's letter is reprinted in Sidney Kaplan and Emma Nogrady Kaplan, *The Black Presence in the Era of the American Revolution* (Amherst: University of Massachusetts Press, 1989), 139–144.

62. Henry Adams, *History of the United States during the Administration of Thomas Jefferson*, 2 vols. (1889; New York, 1930), 1: 144, quoted in Andrew Burstein, *The Inner Jefferson: Portrait of a Grieving Optimist* (Charlottesville: University Press of Virginia, 1995), 148. Malone, *Jefferson as Political Leader*, 6. At age seventy-one, writing to Edward Coles, Madison's private secretary, who intended to move to Illinois and emancipate his slaves there and was asking Jefferson for support in furthering emancipation projects, Jefferson vividly recalled the price paid forty-seven years before for running against the tide of Virginia slaveowners. In discouraging Coles from pursuing emancipationist ideas, he reminded him that Richard Bland, an eminent and famously pious Virginia legislator, "was denounced as an enemy of his country, and was treated with the grossest indecorum" for merely allowing a slaveowner to free a slave without legislative approval. Jefferson to

Coles, August 25, 1814, quoted in Kennedy, *Jefferson's Lost Cause,* 82.

63. McCoy, *Last of the Fathers,* 260–261. Madison to James Madison Sr., September 8, 1783, *Papers of James Madison,* 8: 304.

64. McCoy, *Last of the Fathers,* 234–236, 266.

65. McColley argues that Jefferson "was unwilling to risk the certain loss of political influence that outspoken opposition to slavery must have caused." *Slavery and Jeffersonian Virginia,* 124. This is the judgment of many historians.

### 3. Race and Citizenship in the Early Republic

1. Rogers Smith, *Civic Ideals: Conflicting Visions of Citizenship in U.S. History* (New Haven: Yale University Press, 1997), 167, 165.

2. Muhlenberg quoted in Gary B. Nash, *Forging Freedom: The Formation of Philadelphia's Black Community* (Cambridge, Mass.: Harvard University Press, 1989), 47.

3. Quotation from William Nell, *Colored Patriots of the American Revolution* (Boston, 1855), where a florid account of Forten's naval experience is given on pp. 167–170. The fullest account of Forten's early life is Julie Winch, *A Gentleman of Color: The Life of James Forten* (New York: Oxford University Press, 2002), chs. 1–3.

4. James H. Kettner, *The Development of American Citizenship, 1608–1870* (Chapel Hill: University of North Carolina Press, 1978), 288. Preambles quoted in Gary B. Nash and Jean R. Soderlund, *Freedom by Degrees: Emancipation in Pennsylvania and Its Aftermath* (New York: Oxford University Press, 1991), 112. For affirmations of racial equality and the use of July 4 to attack the national sin of slavery in the 1790s and the early nineteenth century, see David Waldstreicher, *In the Midst of Perpetual Fetes: The Making of American Nationalism, 1776–1820* (Chapel Hill: University of North Carolina Press, 1997), 308–314.

5. Gary B. Nash, "Reverberations of Haiti in the American North: Black Saint Dominguans in Philadelphia," *Pennsylvania History* 65 (1998), 44–73. For the Haitian Revolution as "a critical juncture in attitudes and policies toward slavery and race relations," see Tim Matthewson, "Jefferson and the Nonrecognition of Haiti," *American Philosophical Society Proceedings* 140 (1996), 22–48. Forten must have witnessed the Philadelphia crowd that roughly treated the five delegates from revolutionary Saint Domingue who arrived in the summer of 1793 while in transit to Paris. See Laurent Dubois, *Avengers of the New World: The Story of the Haitian Revolution* (Cambridge, Mass.: Harvard University Press, 2004), 168–169.

6. Nash, *Race and Revolution: The Inaugural Merrill Jensen Lectures* (Madison, Wis.: Madison House, 1988), 78; Winch, *Gentleman of Color,* 134–135, 152–153.

7. Don E. Fehrenbacher, *The Slaveholding Republic: An Account of the United States Government's Relations to Slavery* (New York: Oxford University Press, 2001), 259–261. The date of 1804 is tentative but is suggested by the report in *New-York Evening Post,* July 10, 12, 1804, that black Philadelphians had been driven from the July 4 celebrations, retreated to form their own militia units, and then marched through the streets "damning the whites and saying they would shew them *St. Domingo.*"

8. Forten, *Letters from a Man of Colour* (Philadelphia, 1813), 8. Excerpts from Forten's letters are republished in Herbert Aptheker, *A Documentary History of the Negro People* (New York: The Citadel Press, 1951), 2 vols., 1: 59–66. Kettner, in ch. 10 of *The Development of American Citizenship,* "Birthright Citizenship and the Status of Indians, Slaves, and Free Negroes," does not treat any attack on free black citizenship before the Missouri controversy of 1819–1821. In Boston, at least as early as 1814, white youth drove free blacks from the Common on celebration days.

9. Forten, *Letters from a Man of Colour,* 10; for legislative proceedings see *Journal of the Pennsylvania House,* 23 (1813–14), 216, 388–389, 417, 481.

10. Forten, *Letters from a Man of Colour,* 1, 7, 10–11.

11. Ibid., 4; see Winch, *Gentleman of Color,* 169–174 for a discussion of Forten's letters.

12. One year later, a Federalist-controlled legislature in Connecticut disenfranchised free African Americans. See James Truslow Adams, "Disenfranchisement of Negroes in New England," *American Historical Review* 30 (1925), 543–547.

13. Richard Newman, *The Transformation of American Abolitionism: Fighting Slavery in the Early Republic* (Chapel Hill: University of North Carolina Press, 2002), 48.

14. Coxe, "America," in *The American Edition of the New Edinburgh Encyclopaedia, Conducted by David Brewster . . . The First American Edition . . .* (Philadelphia, 1813), I, pt. II, 667. According to Coxe's biographer, the "America" essay was a slight revision of the original "New World" essays published in the *Democratic Press* in 1809. See Jacob E. Cooke, *Tench Coxe and the Early Republic* (Chapel Hill: University of North Carolina Press, 1978), 504.

15. Ibid., 667–668. Smith, *Civic Ideals,* 167. Coxe took note of the work going on to inculcate in Native Americans a desire "to embrace our political economy, our civil institutions, our morals, and our religion," and the same was true with black Americans, though their numbers and condition made this a costly and difficult process that was "gradual, deliberate, and arduous." But he had no doubt that "the

humanity of our white people" was elevating freed slaves "from their African condition." Ibid., 507; Jacob Cooke describes other parts of the "New World" essays at 504–507.

16. Caldwell became a member of the medical faculty at the University of Pennsylvania in 1810, though by now he was estranged from Rush. Caldwell's essays were provoked by the reissue in 1810 of Samuel Stanhope Smith's *Essay on the Causes of the Variety of Complexion and Figure in the Human Species,* where Smith argued for the unity of humankind and averred that "the Negro is in every respect similar to us, only that his skin, or rather the skin of his ancestors, had been darkened by the sun." For a detailed account, see Bruce Dain, *A Hideous Monster: American Race Theory in the Early Republic* (Cambridge, Mass.: Harvard University Press, 2002), ch. 2.

17. Winthrop D. Jordan, *White over Black: American Attitudes toward the Negro, 1550–1812* (Chapel Hill: University of North Carolina Press, 1968), 533–534.

18. Dain, *Hideous Monster,* 72.

19. Jordan, *White over Black,* 530–538.

20. Ibid., 542–543, 544 (quoting Smith), 546 (quoting Jefferson, *Notes on the State of Virginia*), 547.

21. Collin and Drinker quoted in Nash, *Forging Freedom,* 180.

22. Branagan quoted in Noel Ignatiev, *How the Irish Became White* (New York: Routledge, 1995), 52. *Serious*

*Remonstrances* quoted in Nash, *Forging Freedom,* 179.
Ignatiev explains Branagan's turnabout as a reac-
tion to the climactic victory of the black Haitian
revolutionaries and the campaign of Dessalines,
Toussaint-Louverture's successor, to rid the island
of white people altogether. *How the Irish Became
White,* 56.

23. William B. Gravely's "The Dialectic of Double Consciousness in Black American Freedom Celebrations, 1808–1863," *Journal of Negro History* 69 (1982),
302–317, is the pioneering study of this phenome-
non. The literature on the topic has grown steadily
since then. For recent discussions with citations to
other work see Waldstreicher, *Perpetual Fetes,* 323–
336; and Mitch Kachun, *Festivals of Freedom: Memory
and Meaning in African American Celebrations, 1808–
1915* (Amherst: University of Massachusetts Press,
2003). On white ridicule of black Americans celebrating the end of the slave trade—the so-called
Bobalition broadsides—see Waldstreicher, *Perpetual
Fetes,* 337–344, and Joanne Melish, *Disowning Slavery:
Gradual Emancipation and "Race" in New England,
1780–1860* (Ithaca: Cornell University Press, 1998),
166–183.

24. Shane White, "'It Was a Proud Day': African Americans, Festivals, and Parades in the North, 1741–
1834," *Journal of American History* 81 (1994), 13–50.

25. Parrott, *Two Orations on the Abolition of the Slave Trade*

*Delivered in Philadelphia in 1812 and 1816,* quoted in Kachun, *Festivals of Freedom,* 32. On the early "freedom festivals," see Kachun, ibid., ch. 1.

26. Paul Goodman, *Of One Blood: Abolitionism and the Origins of Racial Equality* (Berkeley: University of California Press, 1998), 19. The ACS has been the subject of a tangled debate over its origins, composition, leadership, and motives. See Douglas R. Egerton, "'Its Origin Is Not a Little Curious': A New Look at the American Colonization Society," *Journal of the Early Republic* 5 (1985), 463–480. A revised version appears in Egerton's *Rebels, Reformers, and Revolutionaries: Collected Essays and Second Thoughts* (New York: Routledge, 2002), 107–119.

27. Accounts of this dramatic meeting are in Nash, *Forging Freedom,* 237–239; and Winch, *Gentleman of Color,* 190–192.

28. Forten to Cuffe, January 25, 1817, in Rosalind Cobb Wiggins, *Captain Paul Cuffe's Logs and Letters, 1808–1817* (Washington: Howard University Press, 1996), 502, and Forten's later account of the meeting in *The Emancipator,* June 30, 1835.

29. "The Protest and Remonstrance of the People of Color in the City and County of Philadelphia," in Aptheker, *Documentary History,* 1. 71–72; and James Forten and Russell Parrott, "An Address to the Humane and Benevolent Inhabitants of the City and County of Philadelphia, August 17, 1817," in Doro-

thy Porter, ed., *Early Negro Writing, 1760–1837* (Boston: Beacon Press, 1971), 265–268. Forten and Parrott emphasized that free blacks were entitled to "share the protection of the excellent laws and just government . . . in common with every individual of the community."

30. *Philadelphia Union,* June 6 and 10, 1818, published in Isaac V. Brown, ed., *Memoirs of the Rev. Robert Finley* (New Brunswick, NJ: Terhune and Letson, 1819). The author of the Dialogues was Robert Finley, president of the Princeton Theological Seminary and publicist of the American Colonization Society.

31. Clay quoted in P. J. Staudenraus, *The African Colonization Movement, 1816–1865* (New York: Columbia University Press, 1961), 28. Caldwell in *National Intelligencer,* December 24, 1816: "It has been a subject of unceasing regret, and anxious solicitude, among many of our best patriots, and wisest statesmen, from the first establishment of our independence, that this class of people [free black Americans] should remain a monument of reproach to those sacred principles of civil liberty, which constitute the foundations of all our constitutions."

32. Kettner, *American Citizenship,* 311.

33. Ibid., 312.

34. *Annals of Congress,* 16th Cong., 2d Sess., 596–599, iii, quoted in Kettner, *American Citizenship,* 313. Adams quoted in Leon Litwack, *North of Slavery: The Negro*

*in the Free States, 1790–1860* (Chicago: University of Chicago Press, 1961), 35.

35. Litwack, *North of Slavery*, 36–39; Kettner, *American Citizenship*, 313–314; Smith, *Civic Ideals*, 179–181.

36. Coxe published his first two essays on November 25 and 28, 1820, and followed them with nine others in December. The final two essays appeared on January 4 and 8, 1821. The essays were precipitated by the Missouri controversy and more particularly by the second Missouri controversy over the right of free black people to enter the state—a measure that Pennsylvania's legislature contemplated from 1805 to 1813 in regard to sealing its own borders. Cooke, *Coxe*, 513. Cooke points out that Coxe was a frequent contributor to Binns's *Democratic Press* and sometime manager of the paper. Coxe continued his attacks on black capabilities in "A Democratic Federalist," "To the People of the United States of America; concerning the Colored Population," *Democratic Press*, February 6, 8, and 12, 1821, and "Les Noires," June 26, 1821.

37. Quotations from the first "Helot" essay in *Democratic Press*, November 23, 1820.

38. Ibid. "New Africa" quoted in Cooke, *Coxe*, 513, apparently from an essay by Coxe signed "Columbus" in *National Recorder*, February 26, 1820. Coxe soon altered his plan. Creating reservations for free African Americans would be too expensive, he decided,

putting aside the question how free black people might have sustained themselves in this kind of situation.

39. Quoted in Cooke, *Coxe*, 514. James Brewer Stewart, in "The Emergence of Racial Modernity and the Rise of the White North, 1790–1840," *Journal of the Early Republic* 18 (1998), 183n2, argues that the 1830s was the crucial decade in the development of "a reflexive disposition on the part of an overwhelming number of northern whites (intellectuals and politicians as well as ordinary people) to regard superior and inferior races as uniform, biologically determined, self-evident, naturalized, immutable 'truths'—and, the development of integrated transregional systems of intellectual endeavor, popular culture, politics and state power that enforced uniform white supremacist norms as 'self-evident' social 'facts.'" Coxe's essays on the "Helots of the United States" indicate that the hardening of white social thinking on matters of race took form at least a decade earlier.

40. Cooke, *Coxe*, 514.

41. "Helots of the United States," #7 and #11, *Democratic Press,* December 22 and 30, 1820. Coxe may have been influenced by the graphic racial caricatures produced by David Claypool Johnston and William Thackera to adorn the walls of Philadel-

phia's genteel white citizens in about 1819. See
Nash, *Forging Freedom*, 254–255. The cartoons used
pseudo-black dialect and pictured pretentious dress
to mock the vanity and stupidity of free black people. Beneath the humor lay the deadly message that
black people were by nature incapable of exercising
the rights and responsibilities of citizenship. See
Melish, *Disowning Slavery*, ch. 5, on a series of broadsides in Boston that ridiculed free black aspiration
to citizenship and turned free people of color into
"counterfeit citizens" (167). Patrick Rael, in *Black
Identity and Black Protest in the Antebellum North*
(Chapel Hill: University of North Carolina Press,
2002), 73, observes that the racial caricatures
"sought to undermine blacks' new claims to participate legitimately in public sphere discourse by
pulling those claims against the stream of progress,
back into the realm of a passing age of patron-cli-
ent relations."

42. Cooke, *Coxe*, 513. "Helots," #3, *Democratic Press*, December 2, 1820. "Helots," #11, *Democratic Press*, December 30, 1820.

43. "Helots," #6, *Democratic Press*, December 20, 1820.
Roberts Vaux and Rev. Charles Milnor were among
the PAS leaders who supported the ACS. By the
early 1830s, when the influence of the PAS had
waned, Pennsylvania had more than eighty local

auxiliaries of the ACS, about one-third of all those spread across the country. See Newman, *Transformation of American Abolitionism,* 117–119.

44. Cooke, *Coxe,* 515. Christ Church, where Coxe worshiped, contributed to the Philadelphia branch of the ACS. The Episcopal bishop in Philadelphia, William White, and Robert Ralston, president of the United States Bank, with whom Coxe interacted frequently, were both early members of the ACS. For Sellers, see his foreword to Goodman, *Of One Blood,* xi. Some of Coxe's language in the essays is redolent of that of Henry Clay, a prime leader of the ACS who argued that colonization would "rid the country of a useless and pernicious, if not dangerous, portion of its population." Clay quoted in Staudenraus, *American Colonization Movement,* 28.

45. Smith, *Civic Ideals,* 166–167. Morris quoted in Sean Wilentz, "The Details of Greatness," *New Republic,* March 29, 2004, 27.

46. Robert P. Forbes, "Slavery and the Meaning of America, 1819–1837" (Ph.D. diss., Yale University, 1994), 182 (citing George A. Boyd, *Elias Boudinot: Patriot and Statesman*), 176–178, 238–240, 264 (quoting Jefferson).

47. Cooke, *Coxe,* 513; Forbes, "Slavery and the Meaning of America," 182. Forbes treats Pennsylvania's role in the Missouri controversy on 196–197, 176–182, 224–226, 239–240, and 264–265.

48. Cooke observes that the "precise effect" of Coxe's writings "is difficult to assess" because "literary or journalistic influence cannot be precisely determined by any known method . . . It is impossible to say how large an audience Coxe's articles commanded." Cooke, *Coxe*, 507.

49. The requirement of property worth $250 disfranchised many free black New Yorkers. Five years later all property requirements for white men were eliminated. Litwack, *North of Slavery*, 82–83. Black Connecticut freemen had lost the franchise in 1818.

50. Vaux to Samuel Emlen, May 31, 1831, quoted in Litwack, *North of Slavery*, 64. Attempts to revive bills to ban the entry of free black people reached Pennsylvania's legislature after 1820 but were rebuffed by those who insisted that the criterion of citizenship was not skin color.

51. Rael, *Black Identity and Black Protest*, 48. The first historian of Philadelphia, John Fanning Watson, wrote in his 1830 *Annals of Philadelphia, and Pennsylvania in the Olden Time:* "Their aspirings and little vanities have been rapidly growing since they got those separate churches, and have received their entire exemption from slavery . . . Thirty to forty years ago, they were much humbler, more esteemed in their places, and more useful to themselves and others." (Reprint, 3 vols.; Philadelphia: Edwin S. Stuart, 1900), 2: 261

52. W. E. B. Du Bois, *The Souls of Black Folk, Essays and Sketches* (1903; Greenwich, Conn., 1961), 141. John Saillant, *Black Puritan, Black Republican: The Life and Thought of Lemuel Haynes, 1753–1833* (New York: Oxford University Press, 2003), 177–180.

53. Vincent Harding, *There Is a River: The Black Struggle for Freedom in America* (New York: Vintage, 1983), 75. Forten, "Original Communication" from "A Man of Colour," *Freedom's Journal*, May 18, 1827.

54. For the fullest treatment of Walker's *Appeal*, see Peter P. Hinks, *To Awaken My Afflicted Brethren: David Walker and the Problem of Antebellum Slave Resistance* (University Park: Pennsylvania State University Press, 1997). Walker's message of black Christians as "a chosen people" was far from new. Richard Allen had used this phrase as early as 1794 in Philadelphia, and Absalom Jones, Allen's close colleague and fellow church leader, had a poignant passage from Isaiah inscribed on the inside wall of St. Thomas' African Episcopal Church: "But ye are a chosen generation, a royal priesthood, and an holy nation, a peculiar people; that ye should shew forth the praise of him who hath called you out of darkness into his marvelous light; which in time past were not a people, but are now the people of God." Similarly, in 1805, Daniel Coker, in Baltimore, published on the theme of blacks in America as "the people of God," a "chosen generation," and a "holy

nation" which had a biblical sanction, comparable to the Hebrew exodus from Egypt, to cleanse white Christians who were mired in the sins of slaveholding and racism and had trapped themselves in the logical contradiction of trying to build a republic of slaveholders. See Albert Raboteau, *A Fire in the Bones: Reflections on African American Religious History* (Boston: Beacon Press, 1995), ch. 2: "'Ethiopia Shall Soon Stretch Forth Her Hands': Black Destiny in Nineteenth-Century America."

55. *The Liberator,* January 22, 1831.

# INDEX